Building the City of Man

W. Warren Wagar

BUILDING THE CITY OF MAN

Outlines of a World Civilization

GROSSMAN PUBLISHERS *New York*
1971

Foreword

War, social injustice, poverty and ecocide are phenomena which mankind has participated in and accommodated to throughout its recorded history. Indeed for much of the time that man has been on the planet Earth and been aware of his surroundings, the vast bulk of mankind has considered these matters to be "in the nature of things." Yet in the last 500 years radical transformations have occurred in consciousness and society: the "natural" has become irresistibly amenable to social change. Thus human sacrifice, cannibalism and slavery, archaic institutions all, have been virtually eliminated from society. Yet other problems of great magnitude persist, and appear insoluble.

Foremost amongst these is the institution of war. It is still a conviction widely held throughout the world that war, springing from aggressive impulses in man, is an inevitable and enduring institution of human society. The pervasiveness of this conviction does not seem to be diminished by the fact that scientific data tend to undermine the proposition that large scale organized violence is a necessary outgrowth of the aggressive impulses experienced by the human species. Our understanding of human nature and social psychology leads toward the conclusion that while man may be an aggressive animal, his aggressive impulses may take various forms, many of which are actually constructive in ways indispensable to the future of civilization.

In this context we should note that the attempt to eliminate war as an institution—rather than to merely diminish its horror and brutality —is of relatively recent vintage. The League of Nations aside (since the United States and a large number of other states were never members of that organization), it can be said fairly that the first widespread attempt to outlaw war is to be found in the Kellogg-Briand pact of 1927, where, for the first time in the history of mankind, the leaders of the majority of nation-states which had the capacity to initiate massive organized violence, renounced war as an instrument of national policy. In 1945 the United Nations, building on the League of Nations and the Kellogg-Briand pact, produced an even more significant commitment to outlawing war. Nevertheless it is true that the United Nations has had only the most modest success over the first twenty-five years of its existence. The present international system, composed as it is of individual nation-states who refuse to surrender sovereignty on matters concerning their own security, now bears within itself the threat of such large scale violence that the institution of war has emerged as one of the great survival problems of mankind.

Inseparable from the future of war are the worldwide problems of poverty, social injustice and ecocide (by which we mean overpopulation, resource depletion and pollution). Each of these has to some extent, different natural histories in civilizations. They nevertheless stand out in the contemporary world as crucial problems that must be solved. Thoughtful and responsible persons throughout the planet have begun to recognize that all these problems are in complex ways interrelated, that together they constitute a systemic crisis of the greatest magnitude.

During the last few centuries two revolutions, the scientific-technological and egalitarian-ideological, have brought these problems to an explosive, earth-wide point. The incredible growth and tempo of the technological revolution has made it possible for one or more nation-states, acting on their own authority, to destroy much of mankind in minutes' time. The explosion of egalitarian ideologies into mass consciousness has led to an unprecedented situation in which demands for justice and improved conditions of material well being are being made with ever-increasing insistence. The prolonged inability of nations to control the burgeoning world population, to moderate the race between the depletion of resources and the long term achievement of universal welfare and ecological stability, to control the eruption into violence of newborn and ancient rivalries and tensions, and to achieve minimal standards of living, is leading to the breakdown of structures of authority and continued widespread, pervasive suffering.

It is to the solution of these problems, war, poverty, social injustice and ecocide, that this series of world order books is directed. World order, then, is an examination of international relations and world affairs that focuses on the questions of how to reduce significantly the likelihood of international violence, and to create tolerable conditions of worldwide economic welfare, social justice, and ecological stability. In more connotative but less precise terminology, the question is, how may we achieve and maintain a warless and more just world.

The series is part of an emerging transnational effort to free the future from the past and to shape a new world order over the last third of the 20th century. The authors contributing to this series share the view that it is both meaningful and necessary to engage in rational and normative analyses leading to the solution of world order problems. Because it is now generally recognized that these problems are of a planetary scope, the authors will come from all the regions of the world, thus providing perspectives from all segments of mankind. At the same time, each author is asked to take seriously the notion of a world interest, and must articulate policies and recommendations that accrue not only to the benefit of a particular geo-political unit, but to the benefit of mankind.

Furthermore this series of world order books, in addition to being transnational and oriented to some conception of the world interest, will exhibit a distinctly futuristic perspective. Each author will thus attempt to build an image of the future he wishes to see realized over the last third of the 20th century. But it will not be enough to create utopias. Each author is also asked to link his image to a concrete description of whatever steps and strategies he believes are both necessary and possible to achieve the world order he wants. The creation of these relevant utopias—relevant in the sense that they permit the reader to understand what would be necessary in order for the image to become a reality—will, we hope, permit a dialogue leading to the creation of a preferred world in which the world order values of peace, economic welfare, social justice and ecological stability are realized on a planetary scale.

Within this broad context this series of books will be varied in style and tone. Some will be scholarly; others will take the form of the speculative essay; yet others may be primarily fictional; a number may reflect some combination of genres. Many of the books will be published in languages other than English. We shall be crucially aided in the task of recruitment and in the shaping of the series generally by a small multi-national board of consulting editors already familiar with the perspective and purpose of the world order approach. It is our belief that the intellectual framework provided by a world order perspective by thoughtful persons throughout the globe, will yield new and powerful insights into the history of man, his present condition, and above all, his future.

We are indebted to Grossman Publishers in New York and to W. H. Freeman and Company in San Francisco for assisting us in embarking on this worldwide enterprise. We should also like to express our appreciation to the World Law Fund for its contribution and support of this program.

Saul H. Mendlovitz
Ian Baldwin, Jr.   *General Editors*

ACKNOWLEDGMENTS

The dedication page names the prophets of the coming world civilization, both living and dead, whose thought has most influenced my own.
Building the City of Man also owes much to the opportunities I have
received in recent years to try out my ideas, in print, in the pulpit, and
from the lecture platform. I should like to thank some of the people
who gave me those opportunities. John Roberts and Sydney Bacon,
who invited me to speak to world federalist groups in London and
Toronto. J. L. Henderson, of the Institute of Education, University of
London. Leland P. Stewart, of the Conference on Science and Religion
and the International Cooperation Council of Los Angeles. Everett R.
Clinchy, of the Institute on Man and Science of Rensselaerville, New
York. Alfred Hassler, of the Fellowship of Reconciliation. Richard
Hudson, the editor of *War/Peace Report*. Leon C. Fay, minister of the
First Unitarian Church of Albuquerque, who gave me the freedom of
his pulpit many times during my years in New Mexico. The N.O.W.
chapter of Albuquerque, whose inaugural meeting I addressed in 1968.
The Center for the Study of Democratic Institutions in Santa Barbara,
and particularly Elisabeth Mann Borgese, John R. Seeley, and W. H.
Ferry. *World Union* of Pondicherry, India, which published an earlier
version of one of the poems in Chapter Eight under the title "The Egg."
   My deepest gratitude goes, of course, to Ian Baldwin, Jr., and Saul
H. Mendlovitz of the World Law Fund, for asking me to write this
book, and for their help and encouragement at every stage in its production.

April, 1971   W. Warren Wagar

With joy and respect, I dedicate this book to the
prophet-fathers of the coming world civilization:

SRI AUROBINDO
BAHÁ'U'LLÁH
THEODORE BRAMELD
AUGUSTE COMTE
MARIE JEAN ANTOINE NICOLAS DE CARITAT, MARQUIS DE
    CONDORCET
GERHARD HIRSCHFELD
WILLIAM ERNEST HOCKING
SIR JULIAN HUXLEY
ERICH KAHLER
K'ANG YU-WEI
IMMANUEL KANT
KARL JASPERS
HERBERT MARCUSE
KARL MARX
CHARLES W. MORRIS
LEWIS MUMFORD
FRIEDRICH NIETZSCHE
F. S. C. NORTHROP
SARVEPALLI RADHAKRISHNAN
OLIVER L. REISER
DANE RUDHYAR
BERTRAND RUSSELL
PITIRIM A. SOROKIN
PIERRE TEILHARD DE CHARDIN
ARNOLD J. TOYNBEE
H. G. WELLS
LANCELOT LAW WHYTE

Contents

Part II: COSMOPOLIS

Part I

THE CRISIS IN CIVILIZATION

CHAPTER ONE

The Great Explosion

1. Know Thine Enemy

Twentieth-century man is a baby in a wicker basket, wailing on the doorstep of Doomsday. He has been abandoned, in all his vile innocence, to a fate beyond the reach of his imagination. No poet or painter can find the symbols to express the truth of man's fate, so much more terrible than he could make or will for himself.

All of us wish to know the enemy of the human race. We shake our fists in futile rage at unknown adversaries, like the foundling on the doorstep. But we have our theories; sometimes we launch into violent accusations.

Here! There! Behold the enemy! It is the Masses, the cattle-people swarming out of the pens in which older societies wisely confined them, trampling on everything fine and beautiful. No, it is the Dictators, the mad geniuses of modern politics, who exploit human misery for the pure love of power. Wrong again. It is World Capitalism, driven by a compulsive greed that has no end but its own negation in socialist revolution. On the contrary. It is World Socialism, the foolish dream of a leveled-down and regimented society that has no goal but the extinction of human freedom. Impossible! It is regimentation itself, the logic of the Machine, which dehumanizes in the name of reason and impoverishes in the name of prosperity.

Well, think again. It is the Nation-State System; rather, the Warfare-State System; rather, Militarism, Pentagonism, the bureaucratic Establishment, the General Staff, the Secret Police. Nonsense! It is the Jew, the maggot in the rotting corpse of liberalism and social democracy. It is the teeming Yellow Man, the jackbooted Hun, the arrogant Anglo, the barbarian Black. But let us be serious. It is human fertility, soil erosion, air pollution. Certainly not! It is the death of faith, spiritual asphyxiation, the end of ideology. It is our Fate, the natural Law of historical cycles, the punishment for Pride. It is the Belial in man, the perennial eviction from Paradise, world without end, amen.

Among so many enemies, how has civilization contrived to endure even this long? Or how can we distinguish between the live weapon and the decoys, if in fact only one of the missiles streaking toward us carries the warhead?

The academic historian, who angers the political activist just because he is professionally incapable of anger, rebels against the notion of enemies. Like A. J. P. Taylor in his greatest *succès de scandale*, a much disputed investigation of *The Origins of the Second World War*, the historian finds no villains, no heroes in his study of the past, even the recent past. But why should the twentieth century, to those who live now, seem the worst of times? What sets it apart from other ages? If we cannot blame willing human antagonists bent on our ruin, or demons, or avenging angels, why have we had to suffer so? Why must we foresee, without quickening of pulse or ghost of doubt, the imminent end of all civilized life on earth?

Speaking as a historian, I confess to a measure of squeamishness myself in all this talk of enemies. Yet it is clear that the twentieth century has generated horrors previously undreamt of in our histories. "A frightful queerness has come into life," H. G. Wells wrote in his last book. Minds are wrenched from "the comforting delusions of normality" by an unsparing question, Is mankind at the end of its tether? With Wells, I must answer, Yes! As far as I can know—although human knowledge is always fallible—what else can I say? Yes.

The enemy of modern civilization is something quite commonplace, and utterly impersonal. I shall not be clever. The enemy is change. The enemy is the geometrically accelerating pace of change in the growth of all the powers of mankind. Wells recalled the golden cord of gravitation that once had held events together by a certain logical consistency. "Now it is as if that cord had vanished and everything was driving anyhow to anywhere at a steadily increasing velocity." So it is with the pace of change. John R. Platt writes of the "crisis of transformation," the steeply rising "S-curve" of change. For Alvin Toffler we are in a state of "future shock," traumatized by the incessant beating of change on our minds and mores. Travelers who suffer from culture shock have "the comforting knowledge that the culture they left behind will be there to return to. The victim of future shock does not."

No man, or group of men, planned the changes that overwhelm us. We live in Michael Harrington's "accidental century." Nor is change confined to technology. The progress of technology has resulted in headlong change in all the material circumstances of human life; nothing could be more obvious. But the progress of philosophy, theoretical science, psychology, and scholarship in every academic field has compelled immeasurable change in the life of the mind and the spirit. Revolutions in education, management, and public administration have repeatedly transformed our social life.

We may not accuse the machine alone, or even the application of the rationalizing spirit to human problems, as Jacques Ellul would insist, although reason was no doubt one of the great seed forces. Faith, curiosity, greed, love, every human faculty has somehow managed, interacting and growing and fusing at ever higher levels, unforeseeably and unpurposefully, to bring human civilization in the twentieth century to its critical mass, to the point at which it must burst. We live in the age of the Great Explosion. We are gasping for air in its first few microseconds, measured by the clocks of geological time. Very soon its fire will sear our lungs. No greater miracle can be imagined than the survival of civilized life in the aftermath of such a blast.

2. Fission and Fusion

"The means of transportation and communication," writes Raymond Aron, "bring the various segments of mankind closer together whereas the means of destruction pull them apart." One could say much more, but Aron points to the most incredible feature of the twentieth-century crisis of change. The Great Explosion is also the Great Implosion. In the language of nuclear weaponry, we are living in an age of simultaneous fission and fusion, of violent forces that promise to tear us apart and of violent forces that promise to whirl us together into a solid mass. The stress upon every body social, and every individual, is intolerable.

Consider the effects of this double motion on the American family. The demands of big business, big government, big education, and big entertainment on the family are entirely contradictory. The family as a factor in production consists only of its individual atoms, the father who sells appli-

ances in a department store, the mother who teaches kindergarten, the
teen-age son who attends the local business college and works weekends as
a short-order cook. Each goes his own way. The law also insists upon protecting individual dignity by making divorce simple and swift.

The family as a consumer unit, by contrast, is forced to fold in upon itself. It consumes a house, furniture, the family car, a vacation trip, a swimming pool, a prescribed diet of evening television programs. With the
emergence of the educated companion-wife who can no longer be rele-
gated to a small corner of her husband's life, married people expect more
of one another than in the past. In some respects the family is more closely
bound together than ever; certainly no man or woman comes to the marriage bed at a greater velocity than the man or woman recently divorced.

Another paradox: the breakdown of organic social relationships in favor
of an equalitarian individualism requires everyone to carve out his own
life, and yet abolishes the barriers between men, so that all have the same
circumstances and perspectives. For good or evil, society is flattened out.
Everyone is on his own, but his own is the same as any other's own. What
began as a movement to divide society into independent particles becomes
a movement to compress all the particles into a homogeneous mass.

Erich Fromm notes the political ramifications of modern freedom. The
free-floating individual discovers that he fears his freedom, that it gives
him spiritual vertigo. Never before modern times was he so free, but never
before has he felt such a powerful compulsion to march with his fellow
man, to form serried ranks on behalf of Class, Race, Nation, Corporation,
Creed. Hence the two great streams of modern thought: individualism and
collectivism. The alienated hairy rebel who glowers in the university lecture hall becomes the ecstatically socialized patron of the rock festival. His
ragged beard is a symbol of dissent and a symbol of conformity.

All this is microsociology. At the other end of the scale, we have the vision of a planet simultaneously flying to pieces and shrinking into a sphere
of fantastic density. Who can deny that social conflict has steadily deep-
ened in our century? Who can deny that every traditional culture has entered into a period of rapid internal disintegration, marked by the collapse
of established moral and religious belief and publicly accepted canons of
beauty and truth; by the crumbling of institutions, class structures, and
folkways; by winds of change that strike at the heart of social order and
call everything into question? What really survives of Confucian China, or
Jeffersonian America, or Orthodox Russia, or Hanoverian England? What

survives of the abortive world order of the Enlightenment or the Christian Republic of the Middle Ages? Scraps and fragments, certainly, like the debris in a city dump on a gusty afternoon; but living organisms? By no means.

Yet the world also grows more compact. Rapid transport and communications pull us together. So do war, population growth, public education, the scale of modern industrial and commercial enterprise, the growth of government, the democratic ethos, the mass media, international organizations, ecumenical movements in religion, and lunar landings. In no earlier century has the volume of human transactions across oceans and continents been so great. An envelope of mind now stretches unbroken around the globe of the earth, writes Pierre Teilhard de Chardin; we are witnesses of the "hominization" of the planet. Her beaches, woods, fields, mountains, deserts—all hominized, all thickly settled elbow to elbow with human flesh, all crackling with the electricity of human thought. A standardized world life-style, based largely on the model furnished by postindustrial North America, struggles to assert itself in every country.

What a confusion! Irresistible pressures crush rapidly decaying local centers of civilization into a precarious new geophysical unity in a world where space and time have been virtually annihilated. Centrifugal force threatens the organicity of every historic structure of life and thought; centripetal force squeezes the broken fragments of these structures into a single, hard, compact sphere of aggregated humanity. Here, for a short while, the one kind of force prevails. There, for a little time, the second. Now one, now the other; or both bashing away together.

Finally, note well: it all happens with sickening speed. Everything is offered, asked, attacked, demanded all at once. During *la belle époque* in Europe and the Progressive Era in the United States—that charming period just before the First World War—poets wrote paeans to the great god Speed, and liberal men everywhere cried for unending Progress. We now have all we can bear of both, and much more. For the decline of the local civilizations has not led to the emergence of an authentic world civilization. The premature fusion of the still lethally radioactive products of their decay can lead only to the big bang of planetary Armageddon.

3. The Feasts of Mars

The enemy is change. The forces of change compel aggregation and disaggregation. With what results—concretely? We may define five categories of calamity: war, poverty, ecocide, dehumanization, and nihilism. Not one is unique to the twentieth century, in the abstract, but the form taken by each has no precedent in history. In that form each has been with us for decades, and each continues to press upon us with no relaxation whatever in the 1970's.

On the contrary, each is more terrifying today than ever before. It is insane to imagine that any of our calamities has yielded to solutions of any kind. The mass media cannot accommodate all of them in their news campaigns at the same time, but they are always with us. Only one major sort of disaster appears to have been permanently averted in the twentieth century. We no longer fear total class war between labor and capital in the white populations of the Western world, and Japan. But this was a specter inherited from the nineteenth century which the nineteenth century, in the domestic policies of Bismarck, for example, had already gone far to exorcise.

The most spectacular of our peculiarly twentieth-century calamities is another kind of total war: the unlimited war of nations on a world scale. All the remaining calamities which we shall inspect later on contribute in various ways to modern world warfare, and vice versa. Some may contribute more heavily in the future than they have in the past. But very likely it is world warfare that will serve as the immediate cause of Doomsday. It may even serve as the ultimate cause. Much of modern world warfare is sheerly political. In the very nature of the sovereign nation-state system, nations look for quarrels, nations conceive of their manifest destinies, nations develop suprarational conceptions of vital national interests. Germany *had to have* the Ukraine, the United States *could not tolerate* a Soviet missile base in Cuba, the Soviet Union *must help* Egypt against Israel.

The damage already done should be enough to dissuade the nations from all further warmaking. Ten million people died as a direct result of the First World War, fifty million as a direct result of the Second. Millions more fell in the Sino-Japanese, the Korean, and the Indochinese wars. Civil wars in Russia, Spain, India, and China have buried other millions.

To be sure, men have always fought one another. In relation to available human and economic resources, the sacrifice of life and labor to warfare in the twentieth century is lower than in many past centuries. The barbarities practiced in twentieth-century war have been practiced before, and with fewer compunctions. But for two reasons we find twentieth-century total warfare intolerable. The first is that we no longer, in the last analysis, accept the old warrior virtues or believe in the cruel necessity of the feasts of Mars. It is all very much as Auguste Comte said more than a century ago. The militarism that seemed appropriate in the theocratic age has been supplanted in the modern age by industrialism. The drums still beat and the trumpets still blare, but the soul has gone out of militarism. The gross inefficiency of war as a supplier of the goods of life, by contrast with peaceful industry, kills the war ethic and robs the warrior of his glory. He keeps on about his business of mass slaughter, because mankind has found no other way to resolve serious international and intergroup quarrels. But he is morally obsolete, and everyone knows it.

The second reason that we find twentieth-century total warfare intolerable is our fear of the havoc still ahead, which promises to be much worse than anything experienced thus far, because of the enormous escalation in destructiveness achieved by recent progress in military technology. Whole peoples have not yet been exterminated, not even the Jews. Cities have not yet been literally wiped out, not even Dresden or Hiroshima. At the present rate of the world's population growth, we replace *in toto* the lost lives of all the wars of our century every year. The real question is, What next? The fact that our total wars have not yet been totally destructive, that tanks, submarines, airplanes, poison gases, flamethrowers, and all the other paraphernalia of modern warfare have not sufficed to wreck civilization, cannot stifle our anxiety. Certain prophets have cried wolf too soon, but they have not slain the wolf.

What are the prospects for the wolf's eventual arrival? One has only to look at the dismal record of world politics since 1945. We must ask certain questions. How many great powers have disarmed? How many countries have surrendered their separate political identities to join with neighbors in federal unions? In how many nations bisected as part of postwar "settlements" have the wounds of partition healed? Who accepts the compromises that divided Korea, Vietnam, India, Palestine, and Germany? How have the problems of Taiwan, Berlin, South Africa, and Kashmir been resolved?

Have the costs of "defense" been reduced? Not at all. The Stockholm International Peace Research Institute reports that the military now spend nearly eight percent of the world's resources, as contrasted with three and a half percent during the period 1918–38. Every year sees a world investment of 200 billion dollars in the various national "defense" establishments, more than twelve hundred times the annual budget of the United

Nations. Has the number of Soviet and American nuclear warheads declined of late? By no means. With the installation of missiles in submarine
fleets, the building of antimissile systems, and the arrival of the multiple in-
dependently-targeted re-entry vehicle, the warhead population steadily
rises. By 1975, we are assured, there will be 15,000 in service, twice the
present number. A single new "multiple" vehicle could transform all the
major cities of European Russia or the Atlantic seaboard of the United
States into radioactive ash heaps. Meanwhile, the ranks of the nuclear
powers have grown to five, and two of these are not even adherents to the
atmospheric test-ban and nonproliferation treaties signed in the 1960's.

But man's capacity for self-deception casts a spell over all these unpalatable facts. Although few serious international problems have been solved
since 1945, although the arms race continues undiminished, although nothing has really changed, the fear of total war has fallen off perceptibly in recent years, above all since the seemingly narrow escape from war in the
Cuba missile crisis of 1962. Some scholars, such as H. Stuart Hughes, argue
that the Cold War "ended" as early as the mid-1950's. Civil defense prepa-
rations, once carried out with a sense of urgency, have been cut back from
the merely inadequate to the patently absurd. When a recent American
science-fiction film, "Beneath the Planet of the Apes," depicted with bitter
honesty the annihilation of all life on earth by a thermonuclear super-
weapon, it was ridiculed in the press, assigned a "G" rating (suitable for
"general" audiences), and shown to millions of families in outdoor cinemas.
The greatest act of violence of which mankind is capable becomes only a
joke; the film predicting it, a comedy for children. Yet if an actress had exposed a single pubic hair, the censors would have forbidden children to attend! So much for the regulation of "morals" in civilized societies.

The truth is that the "unthinkable" has never been thinkable for more
than brief periods of time. It haunts us and catches us unawares now and
again. But psychological defense mechanisms operate to prevent us from
taking the threat of total war seriously with any degree of consistency. The
same thing happened to almost everyone before the First World War, and,
to some people, before the Second. Consciousness of the moral obsolescence of war and the everyday common sense of most human beings conspire to keep us relatively tranquil, most of the time.

But our everyday common sense, in the present context, deludes us fa-
tally. Our protective mechanisms save us from personal madness, only to
propel us into mass schizophrenia and mass suicide. By all the tests applied

in the darkest hours of the Stalin-Truman era, and by others not then available, the probability of total war before the end of the century remains as high as ever. Perhaps higher.

Total war will come because the nineteenth- and twentieth-century international power system remains intact, and because potential occasions for conflict among the great powers have increased, rather than decreased, in the quarter-century since World War II. Some occasions we have already alluded to: the swarm of still unresolved problems dating back to the 1940's, the blindly accelerating arms race. Newer sources of instability and crisis come to light every year, from the growing imbalance of food and population in the middle latitudes of the planet to the deteriorating political health of the *anciens régimes* of Latin America. Although a true world civilization could cope with all this and more, the international system that must actually confront these causes of conflict is a system so pitifully antiquated that it might as well not exist at all.

The outstanding features of the present system are national sovereignty, the diplomatic services (from the smallest consulates to the embassies of the United Nations Organization), and, since the 1950's, a polycentric rather than bipolar relationship among the contending powers. The bipolarity of the Stalin-Truman era, when the Soviet Union and the United States alone possessed initiative in world affairs, proved to be quite short-lived. It was, one might say, "unnatural," since polycentrism had prevailed for more than a century before it, and has prevailed ever since its collapse. In a bipolar system, the risk of world war is statistically reduced because only two powers can decide to wage it. In a polycentric system, almost any country, even one so small as Cuba or Israel, can ignite serious local conflict, and most medium-sized and large powers enjoy all sorts of opportunities to precipitate a total world war. Decisions taken in Paris, Bucharest, Peking, or Islamabad may produce the same catastrophes as those taken in Washington or Moscow. The Great War of 1914 began in Belgrade and Vienna, not Paris or Berlin.

The failure of the international system to make a sane response to the genocidal dimensions of contemporary total warfare is well illustrated by the nuclear nonproliferation treaty of 1968. Quite apart from the fact that many of the world's major powers have never signed it, the treaty remains a meaningless document in the prenuclear tradition because it is a treaty among sovereign states that renounce none of their sovereignty. Consider only Article Ten, which declares:

Each party shall in exercising its national sovereignty have the right to withdraw from the treaty if it decides that extraordinary events, related to the subject-matter of this treaty, have jeopardized the supreme interests of its country.

Does such a clause invalidate the treaty? Not really, since it only defines powers already reserved in perpetuity by all sovereign states. The treaty is worthless because all treaties are worthless, pledges made by wild carnivores still in a state of nature with respect to one another.

In a polycentric international system, where all effective power is lodged not in world organizations but in local governments, the odds against permanent peace are awesome. Sooner or later, the system must "lose." As John R. Platt says, in writing of the "nuclear roulette" being played by the powers: "It finally, certainly, kills you. Some have estimated that our 'half life' under these circumstances—that is, the probable number of years before these repeated confrontations add up to a fifty-fifty chance of destroying the human race forever—may be only about ten or twenty years. This cannot continue. No one lives very long walking on loose rocks at the edge of a precipice."

Nor do we have to stumble more than once. One miscalculation, one accident, one paranoid decision by a demagogue, one crisis that puts in jeopardy the "supreme interests" of one country, and the game is over. Can we seriously imagine scores of sovereign states, entangled in various networks of alliance, glaring at one another across their several frontiers, playing power politics, marching resolutely to this or that brink, over and over again, without once misjudging badly enough to set in motion a third world war? How much luck would it take?

In the affairs of men, who always enjoy a margin of freedom, probability cannot approach certainty except asymptotically. But only if we use our freedom, and use it very soon, can we escape the fate marked out for us by our international system. Left to its own devices, the system (together with the race of creatures it "protects") is programmed for inevitable self-destruction.

4. Two Men in Three

One of the most difficult sayings of Jesus for modern men appears in Matthew 26:11. "For ye have the poor always with you." Jesus here seems to agree with the eternal conservative that no lasting solution to the social problem is possible. Yet, in the twentieth century, Western civilization has apparently solved the technical problems that once made mass poverty inseparable from the human condition. Never in history has the common man enjoyed such a high material standard of life. As few as a hundred years ago in Europe, writes William L. Langer, "droves of half-starved, half-naked men, women and children plodded along the roads begging for food and rags." All that is now inconceivable. *Sic transit squalor mundi.*

Or have we spoken too soon? Is the Western "conquest" of hunger and poverty an illusion caused by temporarily superrapid technical progress in agriculture, soon to be overtaken by soaring populations and a new age of misery? Even if the West somehow wards off disaster, can its methods be learned quickly enough by the Eastern portion of humanity? Charles Galton Darwin in *The Next Million Years* predicted alternating periods of feast and famine to the end of human history. William and Paul Paddock in *Famine—1975!* see planetary starvation almost upon us, with surplus food from countries such as the United States able to save only a fraction of those who must die. If we look at the problem of poverty from a world perspective, and consider long-term possibilities, is Matthew 26:11 so very wrong?

The basic ecological issues at stake will be explored later in this chapter. What concerns us now is something much less cosmic, but of the most terrible urgency to mankind in the years immediately ahead: the problem of the gross disparity in wealth between the world's "developed" and "underdeveloped" societies. Whatever success the developed societies have achieved, with whatever prospects for continued prosperity in the future, the gap that actually exists between rich and poor in the world community is one of the great calamities of our time. Like total warfare, it is calamitous not because it is a new form of suffering, but because it is unacceptable to the modern social conscience and because it threatens to grow much worse in times to come. Men have always starved, but why should they starve when *Homo sapiens* possesses a technology that makes hunger unnecessary? Some countries have always been poor, but why should they remain poor when the means to change poverty into relative affluence lie ready at hand? For that matter, why should members of certain minority groups within the developed societies live only half as well as the rest of the population, when they are all citizens of the same polity?

The patches of semipoverty in the developed societies may eventually disappear, although conditions especially in the United States remain very critical. But international poverty is something else. Here, the disparities steadily grow. Two men out of three on the earth today live in desolating poverty. The nineteen richest countries, with sixteen percent of the world's people, receive more than seventy percent of its income. They consume nearly all the world's commercially produced energy, and they have expropriated nearly all its mineral wealth. Their "share" of everything rises every year. They earn their wealth by virtue of superior organization, superior business methods, and superior technology; it becomes increasingly difficult for societies outside the pale of Western civilization to compete. Keeping pace, much less catching up, are out of the question. The capital and the skills and the social discipline do not exist. Only Japan has succeeded in making the great transition, and Japan entered into active competition with the West earlier than some of the Western countries themselves.

How can the underdeveloped societies reach a level of life comparable to that already attained by the developed societies? How much longer will they tolerate a world economy that inexorably deepens the poverty of the poor as it inexorably multiplies the wealth of the rich? What will happen when the world cycle of famines prophesied by the Paddocks begins in 1975, or 1980, or 1985?

The wealthy nations have not been entirely indifferent to the problem of international poverty. Since 1945 they have sent the poor nations technical and economic assistance with a cash value of some twenty-five or thirty billion dollars, chiefly in the form of loans that must be repaid. This amounts to much less than one percent of the national income of the donors, and does not begin to equal the profits made from their overseas corporate and public investments. Most of it is aid that flows directly from one capital to another, serving the national policy aims of the power structure in the former, and often wasted and misused by the power structure in the latter. That help on this scale can avert catastrophe is madly improbable. By contrast with real needs, it is only a smile, an encouraging word, a polite gesture.

Even if the social conscience of Westerners could be sufficiently anesthetized to ignore or accept the growing misery of the peoples of South Asia, Africa, and Latin America, the social conscience of those who must starve will demand vigorous action. There will be more social revolutions;

new species of demagogy and totalitarianism; and various "reprisals" against the developed countries, whose endless appetite for raw materials will not allow them to break off all ties with the poor countries. What we have seen for many years in Indochina, what Johan Galtung describes as "international class-war" between rich and poor nations, will become more frequent. An international class-war of horrific proportions is already in the making between developed Russia and underdeveloped China. The young Soviet historian Andrei Amalrik expects it to break out between 1975 and 1980.

The international poor will also fight one another, exasperated by their internal problems, and unable to present a common front against their alleged exploiters. In the rich world the danger of fascist reaction will grow prodigiously, in the face of real or imagined threats from the poor nations —who, of course, will not be so poor that they cannot build nuclear weapons of their own.

But make one thing sure. No matter how many revolutions and famines are scheduled for the rest of the century, no matter what the plight of the international poor, the peoples of the developed countries will not voluntarily accept any diminution of their material standard of life, except to pay the costs of total war. Quite the opposite: barring a fundamental revolutionary change in the international system, they will expect and demand continuing improvements in their own living standards. They will insist upon becoming steadily richer. Although only strenuous belt tightening by the rich nations and an immense world assistance program under the auspices of the United Nations or a world republic can significantly reduce world poverty, nothing will be done. The solution already applied to domestic class war, which Marxists characterize as the "bribery of the proletariat," will not be applied to international class war because nation-states admit no responsibility to other nation-states. For the two men in three, the future looks quite hopeless.

5. Ecocide

The disaster of international poverty is only one aspect of a larger problem that the Great Explosion in twentieth-century life has created for striving humanity. When we speak of "imbalance" between population and food supply, when we speak of the "endless appetite" of Western man for raw materials, when we speak of "wealth" and "scarcity," we have already broached the subject of human ecology. After war and poverty, the third major calamity of our era is the calamity of ecocide.

Ecocide means, literally, "the destruction of the house." Man's house is the earth, and he is hard at work tearing it down. All creatures attempt ecocide, in the sense that they multiply and consume as much as possible, heedless of the consequences. But only man, among living species, has the technical resources to make the earth actually uninhabitable for himself and most of his fellow species. Only man knowingly destroys his house, and only man has the intelligence and liberty to preserve it against further spoliation.

The current public interest in ecology will probably not last long, and it will be weakened by the introduction of all sorts of foolish and ephemeral side issues, but ecology itself is no pseudoscience. It has astonishing potentialities for waking the human race to authentic awareness of its common destiny and common peril. Human ecology is a holistic science; which is to say, it studies totalities. It studies the interaction of all men with all of their environment. It studies interrelationships, rather than isolated events. It does not permit that which is reasonable in itself alone, but lunatic in the context of the whole of life, to escape detection.

One of the most important recent achievements of ecological research and—more important perhaps—ecological thinking, is the refutation once and for all of the Western myth of limitless abundance and growth. Intoxicated by our material progress since the nineteenth century, many of us began to imagine that we could go on growing nonstop until the Last Trump. Social psychologists began to concern themselves with the psychic "problems" of affluence, such as the uses of leisure, the new mass hedonism, the collapse of thrift. Engineers began to look for ways of expanding human living space into the deserts and seas. Manufacturers began to build obsolescence into their products and improved advertising and sales techniques in a frantic effort to cope with the tendency of production to "outrun" consumption even in a society with well exploited mass markets. Dietitians worried about overweight, farm experts about food surpluses, economists about inflation and growth rates.

In a typical fictional extrapolation of current trends, Gerald Jonas's story "The Shaker Revival" looked forward to the Abundant Society of the 1990's in America, when Washington will be forced to create a Consumer Corps and issue Federal Travel Grants to burn up excess economic fat.

The Twenty-seventh Amendment to the Constitution "guarantees the right of each white citizen over the age of fifteen to the free and unrestricted enjoyment of his own senses." Jonas's imaginary America is assailed by a Puritan revival, a new "Shaker" movement that ascetically renounces war, sex, and money, and threatens to undermine the very foundations of the Abundant Society. But can neo-Shakerism stop the march of progress and the instinctive greed of *Homo sapiens?*

To all this, the response of ecology is very clear. Affluence may continue to be a "problem" for some time in the rich world, but the long-term prospect is for the return of an economy of scarcity everywhere by the twenty-first century. Eternal expansion and growth violate the basic principles of ecology. When we plunder and devastate our house, the only house available to mankind at the present time, we invite massive impoverishment.

Ecocide involves three closely related activities of modern man: the fouling of the earth by the waste products of civilization, the exhaustion of the raw materials of the earth by ruthless exploitation, and the overcrowding of the earth by relentless breeding. The third, as everyone knows, is what makes the other two so lethal. The more rapidly we breed, the more materials we consume and the more waste products we excrete. We may improve our technical means of exploiting the remaining salvageable resources, but, by what Kenneth Watt calls the "ecocidal asymptote," this improvement of technology only hastens the inevitable day of total exhaustion.

The ways in which we foul our environment hardly need elaboration here. Our cities are slowly but visibly strangling in their own excreta. The earth, the air, the seas, are all poisoned. Even if the earth somehow survives toxicosis, we are fast running out of potable water, oxygen, arable soil, fossil fuels, metals, in short, everything needed to sustain modern civilization. The statistics dumbfound. The Stanford geologist Charles F. Park, Jr., reports that each inhabitant of the United States alone consumes one ton of iron and eighteen pounds of copper per year. He sees little hope—and why should he?—that Americans can continue to use up metals at this rate for many more years, and no hope at all that current American consumption levels can ever be reached by mankind at large.

What is still more incredible, of course, is that the human race has not been content merely to despoil its home. It has behaved exactly like a tribe of rats breaking into a newly filled granary. It has produced as many offspring as the sudden "surplus" of nourishment can temporarily feed. It continues to honor the fruitful womb, tax the childless, and punish sexual congress outside the social breeding unit.

We all know what is coming; what is already too late to stop. As Constantinos Doxiadis, the Greek city planner, explained at a recent conference in San Juan, even if the United Nations were to agree on an effective global master plan for birth control and begin to implement it immediately, our present world population of three and a half billion would still soar to seven billion by the year 2000 and level off during the twenty-first century at approximately twelve billion. That is the best we can hope for, if we act now. It is a question only of whether we get twelve billion with planning, or something like thirty billion without planning. How can twelve, let alone thirty, billion large and voracious organisms contrive to share the dwindling treasures of the planet in peace, equality, and well-being? The answer is: they cannot. In the world as it is now organized, they cannot and they will not.

The impending ecological disaster also takes us back to the problem of world poverty. If the developed countries cannot go on spending and growing at their present rate, much less can the underdeveloped countries hope to do so at some future time. The dreams, in which I have shared, of raising the poor nations up to current Western levels of affluence by means of a "crash program" of world technical and economic aid become nightmares when translated into the hard facts of ecology. Even if such a program could be mounted, and we have already argued that nothing of the sort is likely to happen, the planet does not have enough natural resources or enough room for waste products to maintain all its human population at the extravagant levels of material life now reached by modern Western societies. We could all be "equal" for a few years at most; then the laws of physics, geology, chemistry, and biology would descend with a terrible swiftness, and smash us flat.

Obviously the only solution is to limit all new families to two children, persuade developed societies to cut their per capita consumption of raw materials by at least seventy-five percent, and ask the underdeveloped societies to trim their expectations of future progress by a similar fraction. Equalization—as well as survival—becomes feasible only if the material goals of both parts of humanity are scaled down drastically. The rich must learn to live with less: not a little less, but much less. The poor must learn to live with the hope of only modest progress: not much more, but a little more.

Just as obviously, our proposed "solution" is acceptable to no one. Not one affluent sovereign state will surrender its wealth until its wealth has been snatched from it by force of circumstance. Not one destitute sovereign state will abandon its aspirations for riches on a Western scale until these aspirations are crushed by the weight of circumstance. When the rats smell the grain, which of their comrades could turn aside the pack, even if he tried?

6. The Logic of Technique

It may be good to pause at this point and ask what has happened, and will happen, to the individual man in a world of total warfare, mass poverty, and ecocide. What becomes of personal freedom? Do we not stumble, here, upon another twentieth-century calamity?

Again, we must expect certain paradoxes. The personal freedom now formally enjoyed by millions of people in many countries is something quite unique in human experience. Medieval common law, the philosophic temper of Greece and the Enlightenment, the religious freedom demanded by the "left wing" of the Reformation, the heritage of the American and French revolutions, and the liberalism of the nineteenth century have combined to establish for certain modern men rights of liberty and privacy far greater than all those claimed or held at any other period in the history of mankind. But no sooner had these rights been won, in most Western countries, than they were threatened, compromised, and sometimes even negated by other tendencies at work in modern life.

As a great assortment of twentieth-century social critics, including Lewis Mumford, Karl Jaspers, Erich Kahler, Jean-Paul Sartre, and Jacques Ellul, have made clear, the assault upon personal freedom in our time comes chiefly from the bureaucratic and technocratic organization of modern society. The villain is not the bureaucrat or the technician, and certainly not his machines, but the logic of technique itself, the logic which specifies the most rational and efficient way of doing things, and is then applied, remorselessly, to the satisfaction of collective human needs. Although some allowance is often made for personal choice or idiosyncrasy, the tendency is always for the technical solution to erode freedom and, ultimately, to robotize the beings it serves. Man is dehumanized by an aspect of his own humanity, by the rational powers that distinguish him from the lower animals. Whatever the prophets of dehumanization may claim, this process has obviously not yet reached its logical end point, not even in the most rigorously totalitarian societies. Stalin's Russia could not prevent a Pasternak, nor Hitler's Germany a Bonhoeffer. But enslavement to the logic of the machine has annihilated much of the freedom that twentieth-century man once enjoyed.

Sometimes the denial of freedom seems unavoidable. The problems that technology creates may require technological solutions. When we propose, as I have just done, the limitation of new families to two children each, we propose a rational—but not necessarily humane—solution to the problem of overpopulation. How could it be enforced, save by the imposition of bureaucratic controls and the use of technological devices? Where do we draw the line between social necessity and personal choice? Too often the line has been drawn to accommodate society at the expense of freedom. A new kind of slavery—technological slavery—promises to supplant the slaveries of feudalism and the Old South.

Unquestionably the trend toward dehumanization will become much more pronounced in future years. Technology and social organization grow steadily more complex and more overwhelming by their own internal momentum. Their evolution is also stimulated by the calamities we have just discussed. I doubt very much that the initial response of most countries to total war or world famine or the depletion of fuels and metals will be to collapse in a heap of helpless jelly. They will respond by organizing whatever natural and human resources they have to the highest possible degree. Russia and Germany in the 1930's and China in the 1950's provide the appropriate models.

This is not to say that the superorganized and supertechnicized society of the future will be able to save mankind from the other disasters in store for it. Jacques Ellul's prophecy of a "world-wide totalitarian dictatorship . . . of test tubes rather than of hobnailed boots," with a stabilized population, unlimited supplies of food and energy, and daily voyages to the moon, is too optimistic. We shall have the technocracy, but not the unity, or the abundance. The social, political, and ecological problems will descend on the technocrats with too much speed and weight to permit technical solutions in sufficient time; and Ellul forgets to tell us how the nation-states will be persuaded to accept a world government.

Students of technology such as Ellul fail to appreciate that although the logic of the machine diminishes personal freedom, man never loses all control over his machines. They remain tied to social objectives that spring from the impersonal will of masses and elites. They robotize the individual to benefit the society, as the society collectively defines its goals. Because our national societies have too little wisdom and vision to cope with the Great Explosion, their bureaucrats and technocrats will not be able to save them, even if they succeed in the total extermination of personal freedom in all its modalities.

It is not difficult to imagine the means by which dehumanization will be pursued. The human engineering foreseen by Aldous Huxley in *Brave New World* and by Gordon Rattray Taylor in *The Biological Time Bomb* may be undertaken in some societies if time permits. Gene surgery, compulsory eugenics, chemical or electronic mind control, and the manufacture of human duplicates by "cloning," belong to a somewhat distant, yet not inconceivable, future.

But techniques of repression and regimentation already in existence may easily be put to fuller use with minimal expense and no need to wait for further basic research. Manipulation of public education and the mass media offers vast opportunities for the control of individual behavior. Still more effective, perhaps, are modern systems of data storage and retrieval, which allow governments and corporations to keep electronic dossiers on their citizens and employees. In collaboration with scientific intelligence services, the data bankers of the future will maintain efficient surveillance over all persons in society. Those individuals whose deviant behavior disqualifies them for the employment and services offered by society will be vigilantly weeded out; the "qualifications" for such employment or services can be raised or lowered as much as society pleases, with or without judicial penalties for deviance, to encourage whatever sort of behavior the society wishes to encourage, and to curb whatever it wishes to curb. No "offender" will escape the ever-tightening net of electronic surveillance. Even now powerful forces in American society are pressing for the establishment of a national data bank. Sooner or later, they will probably succeed in their suit. One thing leads to another: it is the logic of the machine.

In the completely organized society of the future, the society of total government and (in capitalist countries) giant corporate monopolies, there need be no jails, no torture chambers, no concentration camps, no gas ovens. But all commodities will be carefully rationed. Only those who con-

form to the norms of society will find suitable employment or be eligible
for most kinds of public services. In time of war, the military establishment
will virtually replace civilian government. Schools will teach loyalty, life-
adjustment, and technical skills. Happiness will be a properly perforated
I.B.M. card in the vaults of the national data bank.

War, poverty, and ecocide are matters of survival. But so, too, is technological slavery. At stake here is the survival not of *Homo sapiens,* the
"naked ape," but of man's *humanitas,* his dignity as a spiritual being transcending all the categories of science and all the requirements of technique. Until very recent times, few members of the human race had any
true understanding of this dignity, or exercised more than a small fraction
of the freedoms it entails. But the progress of human consciousness has
been accompanied by the progress of technique as well. In a world overwhelmed by the problems that technique itself has created or exacerbated,
the logic of technique seems to demand the extinction of *humanitas.*

7. The End of Belief

The condition of man as a spiritual entity, who stands in grave danger of
being despiritualized by his own logic, forces us to consider one final horror, the disaster that has befallen free thought in the twentieth century:
the disaster of nihilism. Cynics might argue that twentieth-century man
has earned his impending robotization. Why should he not submit to the
logic of technique, when he is clearly incapable of using whatever freedom
he still enjoys to believe in anything that transcends logic? Man is a religious animal, with a will to believe and a need to be gripped by ultimate
concern. Yet the twentieth century, as Nietzsche predicted, marks the end
of belief; the death of God. No greater disaster can be imagined, although
initially its effect is felt only by a few peripatetic madmen. Only the advance guard of the intelligentsia are troubled—thus far. In time, every man
will be an infidel, and mankind will weep for its fall from innocence.

I am not at all sure that any kind of civilization can long survive without
religion, or without the quest for transcendental meaning in life, which is
the same thing. One might as well ask a man to live without will and desire, no matter how strong his rational powers or his bodily health. But we
fast approach a religionless social order in our own century. In part, the
calamities of the century itself may be held responsible. They would shake
any system of faith. In greater measure, the nihilism of modern man is the

result of internal developments in the history of ideas—a history that might have taken much the same course without any stimulus from the outside world.

Three tendencies in thought since the seventeenth century have brought about the *débâcle:* the rationalism and scientism of the Enlightenment, which has stripped our traditional religious faiths of their mythology and naturalized the supernatural; the critical tradition in rationalism, initiated by Berkeley, Hume, and Kant, which shows that reason and science themselves are powerless to know truth or goodness or beauty; and the relativistic detachment of modern scholarship, which identifies all values as the products of their historical milieu, their culture, and the psychology of their exponents. These are radical and devastating trends of thought. They destroy old faiths; if carried far enough, they destroy the possibility of faith itself. Modern man, as Franklin L. Baumer writes, feels "an agonizing sense of loss and hence of 'longing.' Not only has God died, but so have the new gods to which so many eighteenth- and nineteenth-century sceptics were able to shift their faith." Religious life is reduced to a quest for transcendental meaning that appears hopeless from the start, in the very nature of things. If the searcher becomes convinced that all searches are in vain, will he not stop looking?

The most spectacular fossils in the twentieth century's museum of dead faiths are those of the traditional religions, such as Christianity, Islam, and Buddhism. Millions of faithful still attend their candles, beads, and prayer rugs; hundreds of ingenious theologians still twist the tortured *credenda* of their confessions into various new shapes and sizes to fit the latest fashions in secular thought. But it is no good. For the intellectual, the artist, the young radical, the free spirit, the old religions are so much ice and stone. The anguished backward leap of a few powerful twentieth-century minds into this or that venerable orthodoxy (the more orthodox the better) fails to convince. Most of us are not leaping; and those who do leap cannot agree on directions and distances.

Other faiths have collapsed. As a society we may have lost the power to believe in the spiritual gymnastics of speculative cosmology, or to create new systems of our own. The philosophically sophisticated critic of the few cosmologies developed in our century, like those of Whitehead and Teilhard de Chardin, dismisses them as anachronisms constructed by men whose world views formed in the period just before 1914. He is reminded of the castles of Mad King Ludwig of Bavaria. He may applaud their courage, but he does not believe. Nearly all philosophers in the twentieth century, whether analytical, existential, or phenomenological, refuse even to ask metaphysical questions. Nor do they speak of an objective science of ethics or aesthetics. We may accuse them of deserting their duty as searchers for Truth. One might as well rail at Schönberg for deserting tonality or at Picasso for deserting perspective.

By the same token, most of the secular ideologies of modern times have become enfeebled, no longer virile enough to attract strong minds to their defense. At one time they served as substitutes for religion, and occasionally still do. But what power remains in classical liberalism, working-class socialism, or the nationalism of Mazzini and Michelet? What life is left in such concocted national "cultures" as Soviet Marxism-Leninism or Americanism or Chairman Maoism? The nation-states and their established orders retain all their overwhelming political and economic power, but they have us by our bellies, not our hearts. Only sporadically, among oppressed or disadvantaged minorities, emerging nationalities in Asia and Africa, and the alienated young, can signs of a resurgence of ideology be detected, and most of this is no more than embryonic.

Perceptive social critics wonder if there is hope for a new age of faith in this still shapeless "counterculture" of radical politics and neo-Bohemianism. Perhaps. But the established order will spare no effort to buy off its best minds. As for the emerging nationalities, they no sooner achieve independence than most of them begin playing the same games as the older states.

But if new faith is on its way, do not doubt that it will be new. Do not expect old commitments to come back in a fresh coat of paint. Look into the eyes of the most authentic radicals, the mind-blown nomads and communards who have voluntarily severed themselves from the "respectable" world. Are they really neo-Bohemians, or is it a deeper estrangement, a reversion in gentle despair to the simplicities of barbarism? They barely speak. They deny our cultures without bothering to produce a reasoned indictment. But if I must choose between the honest nay-saying of the new barbarians, which affirms life for its own goodness, or the official optimism of the technocracy, which destroys civilization by pretending to protect it, I shall choose the barbarians every time. On their negations, we may build something durable. On the affirmations of established power, we can build only the funeral pyre of mankind.

8. The Crack of Doom

We could, no doubt, discover more calamities in the making than these five, but why look any further? What a case of overkill! Any of the five could annihilate us. Yet notice how each feeds on the others. International poverty and the crisis of ecocide provide excellent motives for total warfare. The logic of technique arms the total warrior, and the end of belief frees him from the last vestiges of social restraint. Total warfare widens the gap between the rich and poor nations, devastates the earth, forces more technocratic regimentation upon civilized society, and undermines faith in man and God. The end of belief renders us more vulnerable to the blandishments of technocracy, more inclined to abandon ourselves to ecocide and international class war. The interactions are countless. All of these calamities stem, directly or indirectly, from the vastly accelerated material progress of Western civilization, which has made everything happen too fast and too soon. Like little boats caught in a maelstrom, we spin round and round, losing all sense of up and down and right and left.

It is no wonder that we cannot adjust to this wild tempo of life. Moral ideas are especially slow to change; they stand in imminent danger of being washed overboard. Consider the case of the William Smiths, Senior and Junior. William Sr. is 48, his son is 21. William Sr. made $10,000 for himself today by financing a deal that will worsen the poverty of 500 Brazilian plantation workers. He then cruised home in his steel-blue Chrysler, polluting the air and burning up five gallons of irreplaceable fossil fuel. He ate a pound of beefsteak for his evening meal, although the land used to produce his beef could have provided twenty men with whole-grain dinners of greater nutritive value. He finished his day by going to bed with his wife and impregnating her for the seventh time. William Smith, Sr. is a "good" man, who has done nothing "wrong."

But what a wastrel is his first child, William Jr.! Young William, who left home last year to become a wandering hippie, on the very same day smoked three marijuana cigarettes and refused induction into the armed forces of his native land, which had hoped to enlist him in its sacred work of killing peasants in Indochina. This enemy of society also performed a sex act with another male, and crowned his villainy by telling a pregnant female acquaintance where she could procure an illegal abortion. William Jr.

is a multiple "felon," whose crimes on this single day could earn him a lifetime of imprisonment at hard labor.

Although young William may some day be driving Chryslers and applying the screws to the Brazilian plantation workers himself, his current life style is a warning to the world he inhabits. The only way to stop boats from spinning helplessly into disaster is to seize them and steer them out of danger. Merely hanging on for dear life, or doing whatever is "safe" and "reasonable," brings mankind that much closer to shipwreck. Our ideas, including our moral ideas, must move even faster than our swirling boats. Ideas alone can save us from the final catastrophe.

Is it really so bad as all that? You may be tiring of apocalyptic images. Next it will be "the crack of doom."

Listen! As I said at the beginning of this chapter, there are no symbols to express the truth of man's fate. No rhetorical device is big enough. The Great Explosion and the calamities that issue from it dwarf all efforts to reduce them to words, sounds, or pictures. But judge for yourselves the odds against mankind's survival. This is a book about the City of Man. Yet if we were extraterrestrial gamblers, considering dispassionately the prospects of the City of Man, we should probably be readier to place our bets on the City of Fishes or the City of Flies, than risk a single galactic shilling on this unlikely creature known as Man.

CHAPTER TWO

Half Measures and Red Herrings

1. The Project of a World Civilization

An intelligent species in deep distress does not permit itself to be paralyzed by poor odds. The greater the challenge, the greater the response. In light of the gravity of our predicament, it is not surprising that millions of able and powerful men throughout the world devote most of their waking hours to the struggle against war and social disintegration. The campaign for world government, with its peace chest of more than ten billion dollars and its twenty-five thousand political candidates contesting seats in all national parliamentary elections; the antiwar strikes, boycotts, and insurrections; the systematic harassment of ecocidal maniacs by mail, telephone, and citizen's arrests; the unnumbered best-selling books on world order that crowd the lists of every major publisher; the civil disobedience of most of the world's clergymen, who refuse any longer to play puppet to national establishments—all of this was to be expected. In every corner of the planet, the people are marching. More than five hundred million signatures were obtained for the recent world petition against nationalism and militarism. Everywhere taxes go unpaid, economies are strangled by consumer resistance, frontier guards have lost control of international checkpoints.

Don't bother to pinch yourself. You wouldn't feel a thing. End of dream! Wake up.

If there is anything more dispiriting than the immensity of the threat to mankind's survival, it is the insignificance of mankind's response. Our "millions of able men" have not yet been born. In the real world, the full-time workers for world integration unbeholden to national power structures could all be accommodated in a Vermont village. Their expenditures in the cause would not provide for the annual needs of Mrs. Jacqueline Onassis. The difference they have made in world affairs is too small to be weighed on any historian's scale.

If the diagnosis offered in Chapter One is sound, the twentieth-century world crisis in civilization involves every aspect of our lives. It is a "totalizing" crisis. Although we must—for sanity's sake—allow ourselves some hope of survival, we have not yet resolved to make a "totalizing" response. Our solutions have been piecemeal, provisional, parochial, uncoordinated, and unsubstantial. They are too often conceived on a national scale, although the real problems are all planetary. They are directed at immediately burning issues, in the unfortunate tradition of American pragmatism, which refuses to see life whole and has no sense of the organic unity of past, present, and future. Above all, they lack prophetic moral vision. Separately or in combination, our responses to the twentieth-century crisis project no sense of world purpose or direction. They are innocent of ultimate objectives. They tinker, when they should forge.

Let us confront our situation manfully. The crisis is too vast to yield to segmental solutions. No repairs can salvage the existing international system. No half measures will prevent ecocide and technological dehumanization. Nothing can stay the evaporation of faith in the old gods. In the language of Arnold J. Toynbee, what we see before us is the socioethical breakdown of all the civilizations of mankind—their death as entities capable of sustaining further organic growth. Wherever growth still does occur, it is most often cancerous and self-destructive. The local civilizations no longer function as organisms.

The circumstances give us two options: either to preserve the shells of our diseased civilizations as long as possible, or to try consciously and concertedly to build a new world civilization. A third possible choice, to abandon civilization and revert to primeval anarchy, contradicts the social nature of man. *Homo sapiens* is a civilization-forming animal. For the past six thousand years, wherever material conditions have been favorable, he has faithfully obeyed the impulse to create civilizations. And a civilization—let us be quite clear—is not simply a human community. It is always an effort to unify the *ecumene,* to bring the whole known world under one law and one cultural configuration. A civilization is a world order. It seeks, although it does not always succeed, to pacify the earth. It is the most effective of mankind's social inventions for subjecting the state of nature to the rule of art, reason, and will.

But when a civilization loses its power to grow and thrive organically, it must be replaced. Toynbee identifies three distinct generations of civilizations since earliest antiquity, each built on the ruins of its predecessor. Some civilizations, like the Mohenjo-Daro society of northern India, disappeared without a trace. Most have transmitted extensive portions of their culture to their successors. None is necessarily immortal. But the inescapable task before mankind at the present juncture in its history is the formation of a new civilization, constructed from the viable and compatible components of all its dying local societies, and scaled to the new dimensions of the *ecumene*—the planet itself. For the first time, the "known world" is the planet earth. The local societies are no longer ecumenical. They can no longer keep the peace, give justice, or solve the most urgent material problems of our communal life. World history has served notice upon them. They must go.

It is at once obvious that the new world civilization will not come into existence, if it comes into existence at all, in the "normal" and "historical" way, by a process of gradual evolution. In certain superficial respects, a world civilization already exists, a world technical order that works unpurposefully toward a common planetary way of life. If we could afford the violence and waste that would accompany such an unpurposeful drift toward integration, if we were not faced with enormous demographic pressures, with weaponry of total destruction, and with a degree of mass consciousness unprecedented in history, it might be just as well to sit back and wait.

Unhappily, the tempo of technological progress does not permit historical patience. If we are to make the transition safely to a unified world civilization, we must accelerate all the natural processes of civilization-building. Whole ages must be telescoped into less than a century. What was largely unpremeditated in the past must become deliberate in the future.

We must totalize the search for world order. We must become architects and builders of civilization. Anything less is too little.

How to begin? Although the experience will be painful, and will force us to deal harshly with good men, I suggest that we can best begin by weighing the past efforts of liberals and radicals to resolve the twentieth-century world crisis. Let us analyze what has been attempted by men who understand, at least in part, the seriousness of the crisis and who are not mindless apologists for the existing order. Their efforts have seldom been exposed to frank criticism. They have enjoyed the same patronizing immunity as the very old and the very young in a well-regulated modern family. But we owe them the courtesy of candor. As pioneers in a desperate undertaking, they have much to teach us. From their failures, and also their successes, we have much to learn.

2. Demythologizing the Peace Movement

The German existentialist theologian Rudolf Bultmann must accept the heavy responsibility for bringing into the language of twentieth-century man a useful but unlovely new word: demythologization. To demythologize is to winnow the chaff of pagan mythological imagery from the good grain of the Christian *kerygma*, or "message." But Christianity is not the only system of ideas enveloped by mythology. The peace movement also stands in need of demythologizing. Of all liberal efforts to respond to the twentieth-century world crisis, the struggle against war is the most direct and the most ambitious. Yet it operates on the basis of illusions that render it almost impotent.

The "peace movement" is an omnibus phrase for many different, but intimately related activities. It started early in the nineteenth century. Its most spectacular achievements before 1914 were the great international conferences held at The Hague in 1899 and 1907. During its long history, it has developed three distinct strategic concepts: resistance to war-making by civil disobedience (either violent or nonviolent); collective security through diplomatic conferences; and world federalism.

Each of these strategic concepts is flawed by utopian premises. The most ingenuous is the first—the idea of civil disobedience—although in one respect it is also the most shrewd. At least it does not go cap in hand to the "guv'nor." It recognizes that war makers will not stop making war unless they are strenuously resisted. Projects for civil disobedience range from the plans of the Second International, just before 1914, to call a general strike by the working men of all countries at war, to the current refusal of many young people to accept induction into national armed forces on any terms. In the same category are the campaign for unilateral nuclear disarmament launched in Great Britain in 1958, the demonstrations in the United States against the war in Indochina, the student protests against militarism and nuclear testing in Japan, and the militant religious pacifism of the International Fellowship of Reconciliation. Following the example of Buddhist monks in Vietnam, some war resisters have resorted to self-immolation. American pacifists have attacked selective service offices and physically threatened the Pentagon.

But civil disobedience directly aimed at national war machines cannot prevent wars. War is an accepted instrument of national policy in all countries, to which all governments turn when they judge that vital national interests can be served in no other way. A sovereign state cannot protect its sovereignty without being prepared to go to war or to accept the military aid of a friendly power. It follows that the decision to make war is a public decision, tacitly or actively supported by the majority of politically responsible citizens in the state. They seldom demand war for the sheer love of blood. But they choose war, and readiness for war, in preference to the surrender of vital national interests. Direct attacks on war machines make little sense, then, because they are attacks on the instrumentalities freely chosen by bodies politic for the pursuit of their interests. To stop war by civil disobedience, one must attack the whole state; one must disavow the sovereign-state system, and persuade others to do likewise. For the same reason, campaigns for general or nuclear disarmament accomplish little. Wars are not made by armies, and much less by arms—only sovereign polities make wars.

It is still more unrealistic to ask men to abjure physical violence in any or all circumstances. The doctrinaire nonviolent pacifism of modern times is a counsel of perfection which arbitrarily prohibits one remedy for an intolerable situation while endorsing others that may inflict or cause the infliction of more harm than violence itself. Man is spirit, as well as flesh. Destroying the flesh is only one way of injuring our fellow men. There are situations in human conflict where violence is necessary; in other types of conflict, nonviolent solutions work very well. Gandhi and Martin Luther King chose appropriate tactics for the struggles they had to lead; so also did Winston Churchill in 1940 and Joseph Stalin in 1941. It would be far better, no doubt, not to injure our fellow men at all, to resolve all conflict by never permitting conflict to arise in the first place. But this is to suggest that men become gods, or robots.

The second strategic concept of the peace movement is collective security through diplomatic conferences. The post-Napoleonic Quadruple Alliance and its "system" of international congresses, which lasted from 1814 until about 1822, was an early example of this strategy in actual operation. It returned to life after the first World War in the Covenant of the League of Nations, and later in the United Nations. Although international collective security arrangements can be made only by states, their strongest defenders today are the various national citizens' associations established to offer them popular support.

But organizations such as the United Nations are only councils of ambassadors. The nations have surrendered and given nothing. The United Nations, like the League before it, has not even replaced the regular system of embassies and consulates by which countries negotiate with one another bilaterally. The United Nations has no power of taxation or legislation, no army, no police force, no judicial authority over persons, and no citizenry. H. G. Wells once called the League of Nations "a homunculus in a bottle." The United Nations is its twin. Proposals to "strengthen" or "improve" it are merely grotesque.

In any case, all schemes for the prevention of war through diplomatic conferences lack realism, whatever temporary relaxation of tensions they may sometimes afford. Diplomats have no power to determine national policy. Even when nations are prepared to seek peaceful settlements of their disputes, the vast polyglot lecture halls of the United Nations are often the worst places in the world to conduct serious negotiations. They could disappear one night in thick Manhattan smog, never be seen again, and never be missed.

The last major strategic concept developed by the peace movement, world federalism, escapes some of the criticisms that must be aimed at civil resistance and diplomatic conferences. It does not limit its attention to war-making as such, and it recognizes that the decision to resort to war is political. It demands the voluntary democratic surrender of the "external" sovereignty of nations to a world political authority. Such a world federal government would assume the responsibilities now shouldered by foreign offices and ministries of defense. In most plans, it would also have certain limited legislative and judicial powers. At the same time, it would zealously protect the "internal" sovereignty of nations, allowing them to manage their domestic affairs as they pleased, while safeguarding their sociocultural integrity. The model of world order envisaged is a pluralistic community of autonomous nations.

Most projects for a democratic world federal government feed on a wide assortment of deadly illusions, which appeal strongly to middle-class and middle-aged liberal opinion because they seem to promise security without the need for radical change. The most obvious of these, the myth of "minimalism," is the working premise of all the others. It argues that the only way to convince nation-states of the relative harmlessness of world government is to require the transfer of the fewest possible powers from national to federal authority. The essence and most of the substance of national sovereignty—as minimalists reassure uneasy statesmen—is preserved.

The theory of divisible sovereignty has long ago been demolished by Hans Morgenthau. Sovereignty means full power. Divided sovereignty is a contradiction in terms. Subtract 10 percent or 25 percent from 100 percent and you no longer have 100 percent. Notice, too, that the one power which, above all, the minimalists hope to wheedle away from national governments is the power of self-defense. This is no ordinary 10 percent or 25 percent: it is the keystone of all sovereignty, which alone guarantees to states the possibility of effective exercise of authority in any form. States may agree to more extensive international controls over world trade, transport, communications, and tourism. One can even imagine a world currency, health service, customs union, or space program. But the last power the nation-states will surrender is their power to make war, and the last way to persuade them to surrender it is to send politically impotent humanitarians to beg respectfully at their doors. It is not for nothing that world federalists rarely interest national intelligence agencies. Their doings are so harmless that governments let them continue unmolested and unnoticed.

Federalism itself is something of a myth. This is the constitutional formula by which "minimal" powers will be delegated to the world authority, and all others reserved to the self-governing states. The classical federalism of the eighteenth century, to which this formula nostalgically alludes, is so much cold mutton in the second half of the twentieth. It survives here and there, in attenuated forms and unusual local circumstances, but all the tendencies of the age fight against it. In modern practice, certain powers are delegated to the component states of the federal union, and ultimate authority rests with the people as a whole, acting as a whole through their federal government. Such federal states as the Soviet Union, West Germany, and the United States do not differ markedly from such unitary states as the United Kingdom and France. The logic of technique and the social and psychic needs of mass democracy demand centralization of power. Federalism on a global scale is ludicrous; in a world of nations so greatly unequal in population and wealth, in a world faced with so many urgent problems requiring drastic public solutions, from population control to imminent race war in South Africa (and perhaps North America), a classically federalist world government would be almost as powerless as the General Assembly of the United Nations.

Yet minimalism and federalism are not urged upon us by world government enthusiasts merely because minimalism and federalism would be hypothetically easier to sell to existing national establishments. Minimalists do not want a maximalist government even if they could get it, because it attacks another of their cherished myths, the idea of cultural pluralism.

Nothing better illustrates the decadence and world weariness of modern Western civilization. The myth of cultural pluralism has captivated every pedestrian liberal mind on both sides of the Atlantic. Its immediate origins are obvious: remorse for the blood-stained imperialism of the past and the economic imperialism of the present; the Wilsonian concept of national self-determination; and the anthropological relativism of the school of Franz Boas. Westerners who cannot contribute one percent of their national income to rectify the economic imbalance of East and West are nonetheless perfectly happy to subscribe to the theory of the complete relativity of sociocultural values. It is a seductive theory, if only because it is scientifically and philosophically impeccable, and costs nothing to espouse. It makes no demands upon others, and—more to the point—no demands upon one's own culture. Nothing need be done except to practice "toleration" or "mutual appreciation."

One of the few times in recent history when cultural pluralism received a definitive public challenge occurred in 1946. Julian Huxley, then executive secretary of the Preparatory Commission for the United Nations Educational, Scientific, and Cultural Organization (UNESCO), warned the commission that UNESCO could not function effectively unless it adhered to an overarching philosophy—which in his judgment should be scientific humanism. At once Huxley encountered implacable criticism. As the American delegate William Benton pointed out, the adoption of any binding credo by the organization would violate its pledge to respect the democratic freedom of every culture to develop along its own lines. Benton's point of view prevailed. UNESCO adopted no credo, and the homunculus in the bottle was spared all embarrassment. Another, somewhat less historic confrontation between cultural pluralism and the concept of a world civilization took place at a meeting of British world federalists which I addressed in Belgravia in 1964. During the question period, a prominent federalist spokesman (Patrick Armstrong) rose to wonder if I did not see "that world government will be created for the express purpose of *preventing* a world civilization! A federal world government must protect the existing national societies, not replace them."

At least this lays the issue plainly and openly on the table. The program of cultural pluralism is to preserve business as usual, except for the imposition of a minimalist world government on the community of nations, a tin hat to be worn in case of emergency, so light and so cheap that it will annoy no one.

Also implicit in the myth of pluralism is the myth of "politicism," the notion that politics itself is the prime determinant of public policy. I have already suggested that the decision to go to war is a political decision, and that sometimes it is a purely political decision. But other influences have their due effect. In the last analysis, the acts of a body politic are determined by its values, mores, class structure, economy, institutions, and historical experience. The political decision is a product of the whole life of the society. Political decisions may generate from their own logic certain other political decisions, but the ultimate source of their authority in either case is the public will.

It is this organic quality of politics that "politicism" chooses to ignore. Politicism contends that states may form and statesmen may govern without a supportive sociocultural context. By such reasoning a world government can flourish without a world civilization or a world public will. Whether such a concept is utopian or dystopian, I could not say; it is certainly not practicable in the real world. But it suits the needs of the cultural pluralists, who must persuade themselves that a seemingly minor adjustment in the structure of world politics will save mankind from Armageddon.

There are other myths, of course. One especially cheerful delusion ("functionalism") proposes that national governments can be drawn willy-nilly into effective union through the spinning of a world-web of governmental and nongovernmental international service organizations. All this will happen, so to speak, behind the backs of the politicians. One fine morning they will all wake up and find themselves guests in the same silken parlor of the same spidery world bureaucracy.

One fine morning! But it will never come. Politicians are not so easily fooled. Even if the sovereign states miraculously did agree to some kind of world administration of international affairs, I have no confidence that such an agreement would be enough to save mankind from disaster. We need much more than a planetary dose of Nixonian "law and order."

Clearly the men and women of the peace movement have hearts where hearts belong. I cannot possibly quarrel with their hope for a planet at peace. We can learn much from the tactics of nonviolent civil disobedience employed by pacifists. Good diplomacy can buy mankind badly needed time. The publicity already given to the idea of a federal world government has helped to create the moral atmosphere in which stronger initiatives and further progress toward world order become feasible.

But the peace movement has tended to lose itself in narrow and doctrinaire byways. A movement whose only real goal is peace (*i.e.*, the absence of war) will never achieve it. One might as well start a happiness movement. Peace is the bliss and felicity that we may live to earn if we create a new world civilization; yet, in and of itself, it is nothing at all.

3. Salvation by Science

The peace movement pleads to the moral and social conscience of mankind. It is essentially a movement of the heart. But we have omitted one school of pacifist thought whose appeal is mostly intellectual. In recent years one of the few newsworthy developments in the peace movement has been a proliferation of institutes for "peace research." Other centers have sprung up for research into the ecocidal crisis. Both have quite different intellectual origins from the traditional peace movement. They belong to the equally venerable Baconian and Saint-Simonian tradition of "salvation by science" or—in Alfred Korzybski's phrase—"human engineering."

One of the major documents in the new scientism is Kenneth Boulding's book *The Meaning of the Twentieth Century*. Boulding is a professional economist and former director of the Center for Research in Conflict Resolution at the University of Michigan. Unlike many contemporary scientist-prophets, he has a firm grasp of the dynamics of world history. He defines "civilization" as a necessary but uncomfortable interlude of one hundred centuries between the million years of prehistory and the era of "postcivilization," the pacified, prosperous world society of the future. In his prognosis, such a postcivilized society is easily within our reach if only we can avoid the three great "traps" of world war, international poverty, and social entropy brought about by premature exhaustion of the earth's resources. How may these traps be avoided? What we must have, writes Boulding, is knowledge. Social scientists studying conflict and population control and natural scientists and engineers discovering how to make limited resources meet expanding material needs, will save mankind. Boulding's concept of a "great transition" from civilization to postcivilization, he tells us, is more "like the multiplication table than it is like an ideological position." Our crisis, as Wells once wrote, is "a race between learning and disaster." We require no new religion, ideology, or party of evangelists, since wise and honest men need only repair to "the standard of the truth itself."

In short, once research workers learn how to resolve conflict scientifically, control human reproductive behavior scientifically, and manage the earth's biological and mineral resources scientifically, mankind at large will soon accept their answers. The greatest obstacle to world integration is lack of adequate technical know-how. The same concern prompts the biophysicist John R. Platt to call for the mobilization of scientists in "task forces for social research and development," to produce thousands of "social inventions." We need "peace-keeping mechanisms with stabilization feedback-designs," advances in "biotechnology" and "game theory," and more research in "management theory." John Fischer in *Harper's* advocates an experimental "Survival University" staffed by "emotionally committed" specialists in the sciences of survival, such as biology, geology, engineering, and government. The motto of the new university "—emblazoned on a life jacket rampant—will be: 'What must we do to be saved?'"

There are few limits to the imagination of working scientists. For them, the deserts can be reclaimed, billions of people can be fed from algae and yeast farms, ample construction materials can be extracted from ordinary sand and rock, and surplus populations can live in giant sea-going or airborne skyscrapers made of aluminum and plastic. For several trillion dollars, it should even be a simple matter to "terra-form" the moon and the planet Mars, thereby almost doubling the *Lebensraum* of the species. Going beyond mere imagination, Buckminster Fuller (the inventor of the geodesic dome) has begun the building of a Centennial World Resources Center at the Edwardsville campus of Southern Illinois University, which

will house an international data bank and a computer feeding facility ena-
bling scientists to "predict in advance, and solve before eruption, potential
world problems associated with world resources and bearing on human
poverty and suffering." The only real obstacle to an age of peace and abundance, Fuller complains, is "politics," an obsolete mode of human interaction that substitutes passion and violence for reason and scientific management. Scientists who use the facilities at Edwardsville will be forbidden to
play politics or import ideologies into their work.

It may seem rather impudent for a nonscientist to say it, especially in
view of the relatively lower scores on I.Q. tests of nonscientists, but the solutions to the twentieth-century world crisis of men like Buckminster Fuller are unintelligent. In spite of their mental powers, these men behave
stupidly. Perhaps because they have deliberately and irrationally shut off
the flow of the most relevant data into their brains, they fail to take into
account the nature of the beast whose survival they hope to make possible.

One question alone is enough to bring these soaring promises of salvation back to mother earth. If only scientist-saviors would bother to read the
fables of Aesop! Contrive the most ingenious technical solutions you can.
Develop new machinery, methods, schemes of organization and control.
Hook all the computers in the world together, end to end. Then ask yourselves: who will bell the cat?

How can societies and governments be induced to implement technical
solutions? We know enough already to renovate the whole human race and
all its civilizations. Many technical solutions no doubt still elude us, and
much more can be learned. But the knowledge already exists to solve many
of our greatest problems. The difficulty is that men and their societies act
only on the urging of beliefs and desires given effect by will. Such beliefs
and desires often conflict with one another, leading also to clashes of will.
As Leslie A. White pointed out long ago in *The Science of Culture*, will and
struggle determine social outcomes, not knowledge; moreover, the choices
available to men in any society are circumscribed by the culture of that society. It is impossible to break out of one's culture and historical situation
and become transcendentally or abstractly free. "No amount of development of the social sciences," White insisted, "would increase or perfect
man's control over civilization by one iota." This does not mean that progress is impossible. In a later chapter of the same book, he even expressed
hope for the eventual organization of "the whole planet and the entire
human species within a single social system." But such organization will be

the responsibility of willing, struggling, and historically conditioned men, not of social scientists acting as *dei ex machina*.

Above all, what we must have are changes of will, which knowledge can help to guide and enlighten, but only if we willingly permit knowledge to do so. The great questions of the future are not questions of "how" but of "who" and "how much." That is, who gets how much of what is left? Who will decide to postpone or modify "unnegotiable" demands? Who will agree to alter his whole way of life and thought? Who will find it possible to sacrifice nearly everything he has, for the sake of others? Who will consent to refrain from imprudent growth or wolfish aggression? How much time will it take to accomplish how much change? Can whole societies surrender their immediate advantage or tolerate their present disadvantages for the sake of the long-term progress of mankind? Will there some day be a politics and religion of human survival? Although we have little reason for hopefulness at the moment, the only thing indispensable to real progress is human will. Knowledge, like science, is in itself entirely neutral and can be turned to any purpose whatsoever.

Some behavioral scientists, needless to add, would object that human behavior, too, can be controlled. Mechanical engineers can build the technical apparatus for survival, and behavioral engineers can ensure that men will use it. We have already explored (in Chapter One) the logic of technique, and the prospects for a planetary anthill. A solution achieved by behavioral engineering would throw out the baby with the bath water. No doubt techniques of advertising, pedagogy, medicine, and whatnot can be invented that will "humanely" induce men to work together more efficiently than they now do. Aggressive impulses can be damped, and tender feelings elevated, without any intervention by the willing subject.

But even if one could stomach its inevitable diminution of human freedom, behavioral engineering entails intolerable risks. *Quis custodiet machinatores?* Who will watch over the engineers? Who will engineer them? How can populations that have submitted to behavioral engineering change or entirely replace a given system of conditioning, after they have lost their wills? How can any science, no matter how subtle and thorough, foresee all the major consequences of an experiment in behavioral engineering involving an intelligent race of three or twelve or thirty billion souls?

Our criticisms of "salvation by science" are not meant to imply that science has nothing to offer suffering humanity. Scientists should be persuaded to enlist *en masse* in the struggle for world integration. But they must school themselves (despite their scores on intelligence tests) to function as yeomen, not field marshals.

4. The New Radicalism

If the peace movement is too narrowly political and scientism not political enough, consider the New Left. It disavows the established order; it is thoroughly, and yet not exclusively, political; it is not middle-aged; it has partisans in every country; it promises to make a new civilization. What more could be asked?

Of all the political events since the Second World War, none has generated greater excitement than the arrival in the mid-1960's of the New Left. For anyone who came of age between 1940 and 1955 (*peccavi*), excitement is mingled with incredulity. We had just settled down, so we believed, to a long winter's nap of consensus politics, the welfare state, economic miracles, and the "Free World"; of Eisenhowerism, Adenauerism, and de-Stalinization. Daniel Bell wrote *The End of Ideology* and Judith Shklar *After Utopia*. Scholars agreed that the "radical impulse" and the "utopian imagination" were dead. But the New Left has given the lie to these obituary notices. The new young refuse to join their older brothers in anti-ideological slumber. They want causes and programs. They want revolutions.

In a representative manifesto of New Leftism, published in the *Berkeley Barb* in the late spring of 1969, a coalition of "liberation committees" promised the conversion of Berkeley's schools into training grounds for revolution, the destruction of the University of California unless it became "relevant to the Third World, workers, women and young people," the protection and expansion of "our drug culture," direct seizures of real estate, the liberation of women, armed self-defense against political repression, a "soulful socialism," the formation of a people's democracy, and solidarity with Black Panthers and other movements "throughout the world to destroy this motherfucking racistcapitalistimperialist system."

Many New Leftists would use more temperate language or less overt tactics, but the vital ingredients of New Leftism are all here: socialism, internationalism, populism, a strong identification with the cause of oppressed minorities, and a militant revolutionary ethos. The slogan of the New Left everywhere, and the last line of the Berkeley manifesto, is "All power to the people."

The instincts of the New Left are sound. In a collapsing civilization, we need such instincts. At last there are young men and women who will not play the sordid games of official nationalism and militarism! But at the same time, the New Left has been a disappointment. The poverty of its imagination, the superficiality of its diagnosis of the twentieth-century world crisis, the sentimentalism and infantilism of its revolutionary strategy, and its self-defeating absorption in purely local and educational issues have gravely impaired its effectiveness. It may have set other forces in motion that no one can yet see; but in its present form, it cannot build the City of Man. Despite its claims to revolutionary leadership, the New Left is not revolutionary enough.

Its first and most profound error has been to shackle itself emotionally and intellectually to the Old Left. In spirit the New Left is only another Jacobin-Marxist-Anarchist defense of "the People" against oppression. The ranks of the so-called oppressors have widened, however, to include the whole middle class, whose eventual precipitation into the proletariat can no longer be seriously expected, and great segments of the rural and urban working class, whose relative affluence and fierce loyalty to the established order have rendered them *plus bourgeois que les bourgeois*—more middle-class than the middle classes themselves. In this way "the People," which means the socioeconomically disadvantaged or oppressed, have dwindled in numbers until they constitute a minority of the population (at least of the male population) in most Western countries. But they remain the rallying point of the Left. It is the *reductio ad absurdum* of sentimental populism. What becomes of populism when most of the people are not "the People?"

New Leftists are nonetheless resolute in their attachment to the cause of "the People." They agree that conspiratorial corporate-bureaucratic elements in all countries but those with young revolutions (China, Cuba, North Vietnam) foment wars, manufacture an artificial "commodity culture," battle movements of national liberation, and ruthlessly oppress the poor. Modern life reduces, in the twentieth century as well as in the nineteenth, to a straight fight between exploiters and their victims. If the poor did not exist, the New Left would have to invent them.

Such innocence takes the breath away. In New Leftist mythology, the oppressed are virtuous because they are oppressed. Societies can dispense with elites, which alone are capable of selfishness, stupidity, and barbarism. The masses are relieved of all blame for the dumb ferocity of world wars and the ecocidal greed of modern civilization. One is asked to forget that all the major political movements of the century (including German national socialism) have drawn their strength from the masses and have taken as their program the pacification of class warfare.

To be sure, poverty and social injustice still thrive, intolerably, in parts of the Western world, and throughout the underdeveloped countries. I make no excuses for the machinations of the capitalist or the feudal land-owner. They bear far more responsibility for the ills of the twentieth century than the masses. But our crisis goes much deeper: it is the death-agony of whole civilizations. Radicals betray their own cause when they imagine that all the problems of the present age result from the oppression of masses by a single devil class or devil race. On the contrary. In the developed countries, doctrinaire populism plays directly into the hands of the national orders themselves. Their willingness to satisfy popular demands for a rising material standard of life is perhaps the foundation of their remaining strength. While resources hold out, reformist elements in the national orders will go on trying to distribute national wealth ever more democratically, following tendencies of societal evolution that started in the developed countries in the nineteenth century. When resources are exhausted, no class will prove more generous or self-sacrificing than any other.

This is no time for romanticism. Mankind needs a whole new civilization, not merely a redistribution of power or income within existing structures. Although the new world civilization must be democratic, both in its system of government and in its socioeconomic life, all classes in the present-day civilizations are equally obsolete, and equally capable of leading the human race to oblivion. Witness the sorrowful history of Soviet Russia, where a new governing class, drawn almost exclusively from the popular masses, pursues domestic and foreign policies no more enlightened, and in some respects less enlightened, than those of nonrevolutionary Western states. "All power to the people!"—in the usage of many New Left romantics—is the death rattle of the old civilization, not the lusty wail of the new.

The same must be said of New Leftist efforts to link arms with the neo-nationalist movements of the late twentieth century, such as Afro-American and Mexican-American nationalism in the United States, the Catholic cause in Ulster, French separatism in Canada, the National Liberation Front in South Vietnam, and Palestinian nationalism. These are all movements representing the interests of groups victimized to some degree by larger or more powerful groups. But every neonationalist program labors competitively for the liberation of its own people. When the disadvantaged group begins to enjoy the same privileges and benefits as its former oppressors, it loses its revolutionary ardor and becomes reconciled to the world of things-as-they-are. All establishments need do is open their gates.

The lesson to the New Left should be clear. Neonationalism is not basically revolutionary. Except in the already independent countries of Asia, Africa, and Latin America, whose poor are too numerous (and whom New Leftists often ignore anyway), disadvantaged ethnic minorities may easily be bought off by any establishment capable of enlightened self-interest. If establishments do not act quickly enough, the disadvantaged group may become more militant, but in such instances it will probably move toward fascism, rather than toward revolutionary social democracy. For the New Left, nothing is gained except embarrassment. By forcing establishments to accelerate the assimilation (and hence the *embourgeoisement*) of their dissident minorities, the New Left temporarily strengthens the establishments. By supporting neonationalism, it may also help to promote neofascism. The New Left cannot win. No matter how just the cause, nationalism by its very nature turns inward upon itself and therefore provides no firm basis for cosmopolitan world revolution. It has no place at all in the revolution unless it can be totally integrated into a larger and more powerful movement. Given the present actual strength of the New Left, the prospects for New Leftist absorption into neonationalism are better than for neonationalist absorption into the New Left.

But democratic socialism has always been an easy prey for tribal passions. It succumbed to them in 1914 and again in the 1930's in Germany and Russia and again in the national welfare states of the 1950's. When nationalism overwhelms paramount loyalty to mankind, the result is always the emasculation of socialism.

The New Left has also diverted too many of its meager resources into struggles directly affecting young people of college age: the fight against compulsory military service, against the legal prohibition of marijuana, and against authoritarianism in higher education. This is the most easily forgiven of all its strategic errors, since the New Left draws most of its tangible support from young people. Some attention to these problems is imperative. But for many New Leftists, incredibly, the success of the whole revolution is hinged on plans for the "liberation" of the universities. The

universities take the place of the mountains in guerrilla warfare. They become the staging areas and training grounds of revolution. Students also
erect barricades during confrontations with civil authorities, in the self-
conscious role of citizens of Paris in 1848–49. "If one day one hundred
campuses were closed in a nationally-coordinated rebellion," writes Jerry
Rubin, "we could force the President of the United States to sue for peace
at the conference table." With massive worker support, rare in recent
times, French students did very nearly overthrow the government of General de Gaulle in May 1968.

Because universities are relatively easy to "occupy" for at least short periods of time, and most of the "natives" are friendly, they seem to make
ideal centers for romantic revolutionary exploits. Faculty and administra-
tions tend to be liberal and eager to appease dissent. But the difficulty is
that universities are neither power centers nor impregnable mountain retreats. Despite their undoubted usefulness to government and industry,
any society can survive without most of their services for months or years
at a time. In any event, the established order—supported by the majority
of "the People" themselves—has no intention of financing or protecting
self-declared instruments of its own overthrow. The expropriation of the
universities for overtly revolutionary purposes will be met, sooner or later,
with crushing force and a wave of counterrevolutionary terror far more
powerful than anything that could be mounted by the New Left. For
milder offenses, the simple expedient of the established order will be to cut
the purse strings. Although the universities may offer the prospective
builders of a new world civilization opportunities to find one another, any
hope of using them as sanctuaries from which to launch guerrilla warfare
is, at least for the time being, misguided.

Still more pointless are the anarcho-terrorist adventures of extremist elements in the New Left, both on and off campus. Like the civil disobedience of nonviolent pacifism, the use of terrorism—bombings, kidnappings,
assassinations—is efficacious only when revolution is near and public opinion ripe for radical change. In a country such as the United States, where a
recent poll disclosed that only two percent of the population describes itself as "radical," terrorism can do nothing except unleash the counterrevolution.

Even the new public anxiety over the environment may turn out to be a
red herring for unwary New Leftists. The issue is real enough, as is the

issue of Afro-American or women's liberation, but the reigning social orders can readily exploit it to their own advantage. Overpopulation, pollution, and exhaustion of resources are, after all, not in the self-interest of any national economy. It follows that governments themselves must show increasing concern about the problem, from their various national points of view. The more vigorously the New Left complains about "the rape of the environment," the easier it will be to persuade electorates to tax themselves to fight environmental spoliation. The more public money flows into the fight, the less will corporate profits suffer. The more the New Left is diverted from revolutionary politics, the less of a nuisance it will be to the established order. If the New Left could, by collaborating in this way with the old order, actually save the environment, at least something very important to mankind would have been won; but where public funds and governmental influence are involved, we may be sure that the fight against spoliation will be waged on a national scale, for short-term gain, and that it will have only a palliative effect, delaying but not preventing world ecocide.

Let me say again: any true believer in the idea of a world civilization must rejoice in the emergence of a new radical conscience. To the extent that capitalism and feudalism, as well as racism and male sexism, support the nation-state system, they are enemies of peace and enemies of mankind. Even if one ignores their involvement in the defense of national political power, they breed injustice which must not be allowed, under any circumstances, to survive into the coming world society.

But a movement that seeks to build a new world civilization must concern itself with much more than the problem of social justice in existing national orders. For the world integrationist, many of the causes of the new radicalism are red herrings, well calculated to throw him off the scent. They become useful to him only when they fall into place in a carefully designed master strategy for world revolution.

5. The Policy of the Whole Hog

Unfortunately master strategists of world revolution are in chronically short supply. It is easier to attend to selected small problems ready at hand. The general public, and most intellectuals as well, dither from one issue to another. Now it is Korea, now Algeria, now Vietnam. Petitions for world government are followed by civil-rights demonstrations, which in turn give way to bomb-shelter building and emigration to New Zealand. Everyone rallies around the Common Market; next the Peace Corps; then campus revolution. Every year brings its new approved activity: marches on nuclear installations, silent vigils, ghetto riots, draft-card burnings, ecology crusades. The current persuasion or obsession of every man, woman, and child over the age of nine is readily identifiable by his dress, hair, ornamentation, and insignia, which undergo complete stylistic metamorphoses at least twice a decade. But nothing ever really changes. We do not give one hour or one dollar in a thousand to the solving of world problems, and only one of every thousand that we do give is not dissipated in haphazard, uncoordinated, miscellaneous philanthropy.

All the movements taken to task in this chapter have something to contribute to the search for a new world. I lament only their lack of broader visions and more versatile strategies. We must pull ourselves together, in spite of everything. Developing a master strategy for world revolution means a drastic simplification of purpose, and at the same time a drastic complexification of effort.

Our goal must be, quite simply, a new organic world civilization, a new sociocultural, economic, and political environment for the species *Homo sapiens*, with a new organic relationship to the larger environment of earth and cosmos. Such a goal simplifies our world view, but it does not make our task any easier or smaller. Just the opposite. The search for social justice, personal freedom, truth and meaning, peace, well-being, and the good life are not superseded by the search for a new civilization, but are assimilated directly into it. Civilization building requires disciplined attention to all the needs of progressive mankind. In coming chapters, therefore, we shall have to discuss politics, law, religion, philosophy, culture, human rights, economics, education, ecology, the universe itself—all in relationship to our vision of the desirable future for mankind.

Nothing can be left out, because everything is collapsing. Proposals to repair the old civilizations, or replace them piece by piece, are madness in reason's mask. H. G. Wells relates an appropriate parable in one of his last books on world order. The survivors of a vessel lost at sea have found refuge on a desert island, where the most likely source of food is a wild pig. The pig, of course, objects. Despite their great hunger, the survivors put forward reasonable suggestions for satisfying their needs without causing too much discomfort to the pig. One man will be content with a loin chop,

THE POLICY OF THE WHOLE HOG

another with the left ham, a third will settle for chitterlings. The cabin boy, however, points out that the animal is unlikely to agree to any diminution of himself whatsoever. In such a situation, the only policy that makes sense is to kill the whole hog and be done with it.

CHAPTER THREE

World Revolution

1. The Need for Revolutionary Elites

Chapter One surveyed the world crisis of the twentieth century, and found little reason to believe that the existing civilizations can resolve or survive it. Chapter Two exposed the insufficiency of past liberal and radical efforts to cope with the crisis, and urged a totalizing response—a movement to create a new organic world civilization. In Chapter Three our task will be to draft blueprints for world revolution. Since this is a revolution that must create a civilization, there are no proper models to follow. The civilizations now in being required hundreds of years to form and take root, and although revolutions of various kinds were needed to give shape and substance to their common life, they did not occur all at once or as events in a great coordinated conscious effort. But I do not apologize for my terms. A revolution is a radical transformation, accomplished through the overturning of an established order. It may occur in the governmental order, the economic order, the order of ideas, or in the whole of civilization. We are speaking now of total revolution.

Some readers will immediately ask, "Do you mean violence? sedition? going outside the system?" These are, for the moment, irrelevant questions, which show that our point has not been well made. The word "revolution" still calls to most minds images of falling Bastilles, street-corner oratory, wars of national liberation, and various other exclusively political happenings. Here it means, not something else, but something more. It means the supersession of the local civilizations of man by a true planetary civilization. It means the disappearance as organic or separate or sovereign entities of our Judeo-Christian, Islamic, Hindu, Buddhist, and Marxist civilizations and our more than one hundred nation-states.

Is this not science-fiction? Exactly. In order to propose a practical solution to the twentieth-century world crisis, I must abandon the conventions of scholarship, the dreary extrapolations, the safe hypotheses, the plausible tinkering with existing institutional structures, and put myself in the place of a science-fiction novelist, or rather a future-fiction novelist, since the typical "scientific" romance of recent decades projects whole imaginary future societies, not the future of science alone. But fiction may have as much to tell us about the shape of things to come as sociology. It is more often right, because it is more often holistic.

I also recommend candor about the men and women who will make the world revolution. In line with the discussion in Chapter Two of the New Leftist myth of populism, let us have no illusions about "the People" rising up in spontaneous wrath to smite the Establishment. Young radicals wisely detest hypocrisy. It is time to abandon the hypocrisy of pretending that the New Left and other past or future revolutionary movements are not created and managed by elites. In all revolutions, a few pre-eminent minds do most of the thinking and planning; they make the decisions, and if they keep the confidence of their followers, they continue to wield most of the actual power. Christianity was not the work of anonymous slaves, but of outstanding charismatic figures of enormous spiritual and intellectual energy from all classes in ancient society, whose names are known to us very well. The same is true of the great men of the Reformation, the Scientific Revolution, the American and French revolutions, and Russian and Chinese communism.

When the New Left calls for "participatory democracy," it is saying in effect that certain unusually brilliant and insightful men who have been excluded from the structures of authority demand a decisive voice, and if necessary will even overturn the existing structures to get it. I intend no sarcasm. Whenever men out of power understand the needs of society better than men in power, great changes are essential. Even if all men were created in all ways equal, which they are not, most would still have to follow the lead of others for the sake of social discipline. No established order can sustain itself, and no revolution can be made against it, if more than a small fraction of those involved actively participate in decision making (as opposed to the democratic election of the decision makers).

The formation of revolutionary elites is therefore imperative. We cannot wait for the broad popular masses to become so disenchanted with the status quo that the old orders collapse without a struggle. We must create a climate of expectation in which revolutionary heroes and messiahs will feel welcome, and in which elites can organize and seize initiatives without delay. It is more important, at this stage, to find leaders than followers.

Put most simply, our revolutionary elites will work along three main fronts: developing a new ideology of world order and a new humanistic religion, building a world political party to guide the transfer of public power from the nation-states to the world republic, and providing survival insurance for civilization against the risk of Doomsday. Let us stretch our minds and see how—just possibly, against all odds, in the teeth of fear and apathy and vested interests—such astonishing things may be done.

2. Toward an Ideology of World Integration

Great as our desire may be to fly to immediate direct action, the movement for a world civilization in the next few years will devote itself almost entirely to thought and discussion. From spoons and bombs to cities and empires, all things man-made are constructed of ideas. All human action not purely reflexive originates in thought. Too many liberals and radicals in search of solutions for the twentieth-century world crisis want to move too fast, for the sheer sake of motion. They are like the world federalist who complained in a letter to me, after learning that I planned to write this book, "But how many others have already been written? To whom will yours be addressed—the converted elite, the unconverted potential elite, the masses? If it's to an elite, hasn't it all been done before? If it's to the masses, wouldn't it be better to *form* a political party?"

His irritation is forgivable. A literature on various aspects of the problem of world order has grown up during the past half century which might fill several longish shelves, most of it concerned with international law, disarmament, world government, and the like. But can we seriously argue that this literature contains much durable writing? Has it inspired the majority of intellectuals to active commitment or devoted adequate thought to the problem of a world civilization—as opposed to a world rule of law? In proportion to the magnitude of the work that must be done to unify mankind, the available literature is no more than a fumbling beginning. Yet, like socialism and nationalism before it, cosmopolitanism can achieve nothing until it produces a full-blown ideology, a program of ideas and values pointing to one or several clearly envisioned desirable futures.

The first prophets of an integrated world civilization in the modern era were thinkers such as the Marquis de Condorcet, Immanuel Kant, Auguste Comte, and H. G. Wells, who approached the problem entirely from a Christian or post-Christian Western point of view. They had a Chinese counterpart in Sun Yat-sen's contemporary, the Confucian scholar-reformer K'ang Yu-wei. As prophets of world order these were all rather isolated figures, despite their great influence and reputation in other roles.

But in the 1940's and 1950's a generation of cosmopolitan thinkers emerged, many of them already in middle age, who laid the foundations for the work that staggers forward today, including this book. There were times, especially in the last years of the Forties, when it seemed as if their movement might pass the "take-off" point, but that point was never reached. I am thinking now of the cosmopolitan social philosophies of Arnold Toynbee, Julian Huxley, Lancelot Law Whyte, Pierre Teilhard de Chardin, Dane Rudhyar, Erich Kahler, Lewis Mumford, Oliver Reiser, F. S. C. Northrop, William Ernest Hocking, Sri Aurobindo, Sarvepalli Radhakrishnan, and several others; and also the campaign for a world federal government and a world legal order, which enlisted men such as Norman Cousins, Emery Reves, Cord Meyer, Jr., Grenville Clark, Louis B. Sohn, Frederick L. Schuman, Robert M. Hutchins, Stringfellow Barr, G. A. Borgese, Lionel Curtis, and Henry Usborne.

There are no fools, charlatans, or weak minds among these philosophers and publicists of world order. Some of them would deserve inclusion on any list of the century's greatest thinkers. But do their collected works contain a thoroughgoing ideology of world integration? I think not. Most federalists, as we pointed out in Chapter Two, fall far short of a doctrine of world civilization, and deliberately so. Their vision seldom goes further than world law and government. The more comprehensive prophetic statements of Toynbee, Teilhard de Chardin, Mumford, and several others clearly anticipate a world civilization, but in each case the prophet's public reputation is based on other work. Toynbee is known as a sociologist of world history, Teilhard de Chardin as a Catholic seer and mystic, Mumford as a student of cities and technics, Whyte as a philosopher of science, and so on. Their concepts of world civilization are mostly scattered through writings which focus on other problems. Only very rarely, as in Northrop's *The Meeting of East and West*, Mumford's *The Transforma-*

tions of Man, Hocking's *The Coming World Civilization,* or Rudhyar's *The Planetarization of Consciousness,* has a prophet dedicated a whole book to his vision of world order.

Still more disheartening is the silence of the last ten or fifteen years. Since the 1950's, instead of gaining momentum, world federalism has steadily declined, and no new generation of cosmopolitan social philosophers has arrived to take the place of the Toynbees and Mumfords. An ideology without new thinkers and new thought, an ideology tied to nothing more than its own ambiguous past, is on the brink of death. If I did not know, in my bones, that the cosmopolitan cause is inseparable from man's future and all hopes for man's salvation, I would have long since abandoned it myself. As Gustav Mahler used to say of his music, before anyone chose to take it seriously, "its time will come." The only danger is that when the "time" comes for a powerful and living ideology of world integration, we may not have enough clock time left to carry out its program.

But some of the fundamental premises of such an ideology are already tolerably clear. As nationalism demands unqualified loyalty to the nation, Marxism to the working class, and Christianity to its Biblical God, so cosmopolitanism—the ideology of world integration—will demand unqualified loyalty to mankind, against the claims of all segmental polities, tribes, and churches. It must be, although not in Jacques Maritain's sense, an *integral humanism.* I am well aware that "unqualified loyalty to mankind" is a phrase open to numerous interpretations; it seems vague, it permits conflicting secondary loyalties, it fails to define mankind. But all ideologies rotate around an axis. Although most of them find a place for mankind, in both theory and practice other loyalties (to state, church, party, community, race, class, family) take precedence. For cosmopolitans, mankind itself is the axis, and I think this will produce in time a true "transvaluation of all values," a radical shift of perspectives that will revolutionize both our way of seeing the world and the world we see.

With mankind as its axis, cosmopolitanism will develop a program for social action whose single overarching purpose is the building of a unified world civilization. Our coming civilization can be nothing less than a complete organism: a unitary world republic nurtured by a new world culture. Cosmopolitanism prescribes creation, not compromise. It is a program for creating a new culture, not for patching up the old cultures; for creating an integrated world commonwealth, not for spinning a denser web of treaties among the old states. Cosmopolitanism explicitly rejects the liberal

goals of cultural pluralism and international federalism because its axis is
mankind. We shall pursue these points further in Chapter Four.

Another ingredient of an ideology of world integration is likely to be
personalism. The life of man is both social and personal. Whether he gives
his ultimate allegiance as a social animal to a small village, a nation-state,
or the world republic, he retains a second fealty at this other pole of his
being—his allegiance to himself. The tension between the two is sometimes almost unbearable, but each presupposes the other. Mankind is its
persons, and the persons are mankind. A mankind that consisted only of artifacts and cultural patterns would be dead, and a person who had nothing
but his naked body would be less than an ape.

The competition between the needs of sociality and personality, which
marks especially modern Western civilization, will not disappear in the
world civilization, but I suspect that it will become much less acute, and
that the world order may be far less intolerant of unconforming personal
behavior than are the local orders. The local orders must develop a high
degree of social solidarity at the expense of personal freedom, because they
are jungle animals, vying with their fellow beasts for land, wealth, power,
the means of subsistence and the symbols of glory. Theirs is a struggle
quite literally to the death. In a pacified world, most men would still seek
to conform to their social environment, as they have always done, but the
exceptional man, the maverick, would no longer appear as a serious threat
to the security of the social organism.

In any event, it is inconceivable that the new cosmopolitanism will not
insist on respect for the freedom, dignity, and integrity of the person to the
maximum extent compatible with societal need. Only in modern times has
personality achieved full self-consciousness and demanded such respect.
But its demands are heard now in all nations and cultures, and the world
civilization, if it speaks for mankind in its twofold being, social and personal, will not seek to reimpose the ancient anonymity of tribalism.
Whether we may also expect the evolution of the "superconsciousness"
prophesied by Gerald Heard and Pierre Teilhard de Chardin—a racial collective mind in which mankind achieves psychic unity through the voluntary union of each personal consciousness with every other, a union preserving and yet transcending the person—is something quite different; but
as the project of freely willing persons, it is not in itself antipersonalist.

In one sense, however, the world civilization will indeed constitute a
new and higher organic manifestation of personal consciousness. It will be

nothing if it is not the expression of a world will, a planetary patriotism of the heart and spirit. As the ideology of world integration unfolds, it must seek attunement with the inner psychic life of man. The great preoccupation of devotees of world order with constitution writing, computer programming, and model building is well and good. But let us not forget that a civilization is above all a richly involuted and introverted complex of psychic energy. It thrives on ideas, and on ideas given deeper resonance by their translation into a variety of symbolic languages. Finding powerful symbols of world integration will be even more difficult than putting our thoughts into words. We need a *thesaurus sanctorum*, a store of holies, to eke out the merely verbal gospel. But such things cannot be manufactured to order.

Finally, an ideology of world integration will incorporate into itself the best elements of modern social democracy. This does not mean the dictatorship of the Gallup poll or the Nielsen rating, of the demagogue or the armed mob, but representative government, judicial due process, equitable distribution of wealth, and public or cooperative ownership of the means of production. These are all elastic phrases, and we shall have to elaborate on them later, in Chapter Seven; but an integralist and personalist cosmopolitanism could not be true to itself if it were not also, in some degree, socialist and democratic.

3. From Ideology to Religion

At some point in its evolution, the ideology of world integration will find part of itself undergoing a rare and mysterious transfiguration; it will cease to be merely a deeply felt system of social values, or a program of social action; it will become a religion, from which—still later—may emerge the civil religion of the world republic.

The religionless society of modern bureaucratic man is a necessary transitional order between the dead theocracies of the past and the sacral-fraternal world civilization of the possible future. We had to destroy, and destroy by "tolerating" and "respecting," the old faiths before we could summon up the energy to find anything better. Our modern places of worship, which Nietzsche's madman called the tombs of God, are today much less terrifying than tombs. They are museums, which some of us visit regularly, to pay our respects in a spirit of bemused and sometimes academic tolerance, as we would wander through halls populated with stuffed elephants and wired dinosaurs.

But I do not think we have outgrown our need for religion, and the movement for a new world civilization will respond to it. Religion is man's way of binding himself to the universe. In Paul Tillich's phrase, it is "ultimate concern." It differs from ideological belief in its greater scope and its inward depths. It ties us to whatever in our perception is ultimately or intrinsically real. In so doing, it makes life coherent, meaningful, consistent; and fortifies us against incidental griefs and injuries and confusions. Sometimes an ideology can do service as a religion, but for mankind as a whole, certainly for a civilization that hopes to minister to every human being on the planet, religion is indispensable. We shall not reach, nor can we sustain, an organic world civilization without the help of a new living religious faith.

This is perhaps the greatest scandal (*skandalon*, "stumbling block") of cosmopolitanism, as opposed to the insipid internationalism of the peace movement. Religionless modern men are embarrassed to speak of religion. They hesitate to offend gratuitously the still powerful ecclesiastical establishments. They suppose that religious faith is necessarily faith in an ancient mythical-supernaturalist world view. Above all, they think they can live without such faith.

I would agree that when religion is defined as obedience to creeds formulated in premodern times, it loses its relevance to contemporary society and to the movement for a world civilization. As Rudolf Bultmann has shown, modern men cannot think in the religious images current in antiquity. But Bultmann and others have not carried their demands for "demythologization" far enough. To demythologize, secularize, or otherwise purge an ancient faith of its imagery, its thought forms, and even the moral and philosophical ideas assimilated from its historical milieu, is not to purify such a faith, but to kill it. Clinging to the empty rites, words, and traditions of a demythologized religion is a type of spiritual necrophilia. More logically, demythologization should be followed by the clothing of the stripped bones of the religious impulse with new flesh: the creation of a new religion.

But how does one "create" a new religion? Could a committee of venerable world religious leaders, or a team of sociologists of religion, or a battery of computers perform such a feat? Perhaps a single great philosopher,

sealed in his study with a month's supply of hallucinogens? There are prec-
edents. Auguste Comte proposed an elaborate "religion of humanity," with
himself as High Priest, which survived its founder and attracted several
hundred devotees in France, England, and Latin America during the second half of the nineteenth century. In a more traditional way, the Persian
prophet Bahá'u'lláh founded the Bahá'í faith in the 1860's, a synthesis of
the major world religions most strongly influenced by Islam and reinforced
by direct "revelations" from God to Bahá'u'lláh himself. Unlike Comte's
religion, Bahá'í is rigorously supernaturalist, but in both faiths the ultimate
aim is world integration on a basis of spiritual values, whether love for the
"Great Being of Humanity," or love of a transcendent Father-God. The
Unitarian-Universalist churches in the English-speaking countries tend in
the same direction, leaning rather closer to Comte than to Bahá'u'lláh. The
international Humanist and Ethical Culture movement is a world religion,
too, although most of its adherents would prefer another term.

Any of these might conceivably become the religion of the new world
civilization itself. Christianity, Islam, Buddhism, and Hinduism also have
ecumenical ambitions, still not entirely extinct, which could be infused
with new energy through the appearance of strenuously evangelical new
sects on the model of Mormonism in the United States or the Soka Gakkai
movement in Japanese Buddhism. Formulas for the union of the traditional
faiths or the creation of a new world religion incorporating the essences of
the old faiths have been suggested by Arnold Toynbee, William Ernest
Hocking, Gerald Heard, and Charles Morris.

But I doubt that the religion of the world civilization will be a product
of scientific research or a committee of scholars. It will not spring from the
recipes of philosophers of religion. I am reluctant to believe that it can
arise through the massive rejuvenation of one of the traditional religions, or
from any "revealed" or supernaturalist faith. Nor do previous attempts to
create a humanistic and naturalistic religion have the imaginative and
evangelical power to become world confessions.

It is far more probable that the movement for a world civilization itself
will give birth to a universal religious faith. In Chapter Four, we shall do
our best to imagine such a religion in being. But we can all encourage its
coming by the simple act of expecting it. As with the need for heroes and
symbols, we must create a climate of expectation in which religious inspi-
ration is credible, and religious leadership welcome.

Such a religion will not force us back into the fantastic thought world of supernaturalist mythology. In its search for coherence, it will discover new ways of orchestrating personhood, mankind, and cosmos. It will set forth a new kind of unified field theory that can restore to life its lost sense of wholeness and goodness. Gods, angels, heavens, cycles of reincarnation, and orders of transcendence will fade in its stronger light. The real world is itself transcendent, when it is seen integrally, as a holistic and dynamic system. The secular is itself sacred.

The new universal religion will also generate ritual forms of its own, styles of reverence and interpersonal union, of which the group therapy marathons and rock festivals of our own time may be crude anticipations. A religion must bind heart, mind, and body, the totality of the self and of mankind, or it will fail and go under.

4. The World Party

Although politics is by no means the whole essence of a revolution that must create a civilization, the world revolution cannot be unpolitical. It will work to establish new political structures, it will oppose old political structures, and it will be unashamedly and defiantly political in all its labors, from first to last. We can recognize no separation between our "church" and our "state."

In its political, as in its spiritual dimension, the movement for a world civilization must adopt strategies that are both radical and serious-minded. Although I am no Leninist, there is much to be learned from Lenin's approach to the problem of revolution: his willingness to study and think, his grasp of world history, his rejection of the anarchism and irresponsible gypsy radicalism of his time, his democratic elitism. In his own way Lenin was as good a Fabian as Sidney Webb. Like old Quintus Fabius Maximus, the archfoe of Hannibal, both Webb and Lenin preferred patient harassment to premature head-on collisions with an enemy still too great to meet on his own ground. Eventually Lenin struck. His timing was right, but he would have waited to the end of his life if the unforeseeable opportunity of the World War had not called him to action.

But partly because of Lenin, and also because of the failures of Lenin's (and Webb's) heirs, the political front of the movement for a world civilization will begin its work with little help from existing world political institutions. The Communist International (Comintern), founded by Lenin and his comrades, was briefly a world revolutionary party, but it soon became an obvious instrument of Soviet Russian foreign policy and was dissolved during the second World War by Stalin. With the postwar defections of the communist parties of Yugoslavia, China, Albania, Rumania, and other countries from Soviet control, international communism has lost even its outward show of monolithic unity and has fully succumbed to the politics of nationalism. The Socialist (or "Second") International still exists, with some forty democratic socialist parties from the noncommunist world as members, but here too the national principle has overwhelmed the internationalist impulses of the original nineteenth-century movement, and the S.I. will doubtless have little to offer the world revolution.

There is also the United Nations. For a few short years during the secretary-generalship of Dag Hammarskjöld, some of us entertained the forlorn hope that perhaps the permanent offices of the United Nations could become politicized, taking advantage of the American-Soviet deadlock to enter world politics as a third force, imposing its own will in the name of humanity. The United Nations action in the Congo seemed at first to foreshadow such a possibility. Much depended on the attitude of the more powerful neutral states.

Even now one can imagine a permanent United Nations peace-keeping force of half a million men, supplied and financed by countries such as Ireland, Sweden, Yugoslavia, Ceylon, and Burma, a force ready to fly at a moment's notice to any scene of armed conflict in the world, compel a cease-fire, and require the combatants to submit their dispute to arbitration by the World Court. These same countries could also agree to provide the funds for a tenfold expansion of United Nations technical and economic assistance programs. The recently established United Nations Volunteers might in time grow large enough to supplant entirely the various national service corps, creating a world brotherhood of denationalized youth. Little by little, the United Nations would annex the power of the national states without any need for a separate world political movement.

But this is dream-stuff. As we pointed out in Chapter Two, the United Nations lacks effective political authority and cannot become a world government without the overthrow of the reigning international system. The lessons learned from the Congolese venture were chiefly negative; no precedent was set. The neutral states have no *esprit de corps* among themselves and no stronger sense of responsibility to mankind at large than the aligned states. Nor will the further expansion of the bureaucracy of the United Nations contribute in any measurable way to its politicization: the United Nations is hopelessly unpolitical, because it represents states, not peoples.

The solution is difficult, but quite obvious. To bring into being an authentic world government, we must first bring into being an authentic world political party. Since none exists, none can be infiltrated and taken over. I am thinking of an entirely new party. Since few existing national states are likely to surrender their sovereignties peacefully and many will not permit the lawful existence of such a party, it will have to be a revolutionary party, with underground as well as above-ground organizations, and the heart and stomach to defend itself against repression.

Something of its spirit is anticipated in a recent article by the Rev. G. Gray Grant, a Jesuit philosopher and a member of the Executive Committee of the World Association of World Federalists. Responding to an article of my own on the bankruptcy of the peace movement, Grant agrees that political problems demand political solutions. Federalists must "face the fact that if they are to achieve their goal they will have to become a radically different kind of organization from what they are today." Youth, he continues, see more clearly than their respectable elders "the falsity, the hypocrisy and the murderous tendencies with which the virus of sovereignty has infected our societies." If the world federalist movement were to fall into the hands of radical youth, as perhaps it should, they would quickly strip it of "its vagueness and its ambiguities, of its timidity and its coziness with governmental authority." It would become nothing less than an instrument of revolutionary direct action.

I have no hope that the World Association of World Federalists can itself become the world party. The surgical techniques required to transmute pigeons into eagles have not yet been invented. But when world federalist executive committeemen can write in this vein, the world party may not be long in coming. A world political party has also been suggested by Richard Hudson, the editor of *War/Peace Report* in New York. Hudson has in mind a conventional democratic party, whose main task would be the election of candidates to public office in the governments of various national states. Certainly this is a start in the right direction, in nations that would tolerate such a party.

But the political arm of a revolutionary movement for world integration will have to become much more than a conventional democratic party. It will function on several planes of political action at one and the same time, taking whatever institutional forms local conditions and opportunities require. In some countries it may be able to limit all or most of its activity to electoral politics. In others, it may be deeply subterranean and unambiguously subversive. In still others, it may concentrate on permeation of governmental and economic elites. There may be countries in which it executes all three strategies simultaneously, operating through a variety of organizational structures in close secret collaboration with one another. As much as possible, such structures will overlap and interact with counterparts in other countries.

I also endorse Grant's intuition that the manpower of the new party must come from new men. Its leaders will be men and women who are, at this writing, still very young or not yet alive. There is no magic or innocence in youth. But people born since the Second World War and the nuclear devastation of Hiroshima and Nagasaki have a perspective on human affairs unavailable to older generations. They know what is possible. They have known it from earliest childhood. Many of them feel no deep filial piety toward the traditional civilizations, which they hold responsible for the predicament of modern man. They are not impressed by the exhortations of their elders to pray for peace, respect the law, attend the church of their choice, and preserve the virginity of their dossiers.

It follows that the most plausible nurseries of world revolutionary politics will be the universities. Academic institutions are not power centers, but they can give power to those who use them seriously. Through a well-chosen program of academic courses and skillful exploitation of the university's research facilities, the aggressive student can acquire systematic knowledge of the world he must change. Students and faculty in many disciplines can organize research programs designed to discover more about the nature of social change, and to stimulate creative speculation about the nature of a world society. Still more important, the university is the most logical starting point in the social process that leads to the formation of revolutionary elites. Here free minds of high caliber can meet one another and make lasting liaisons. All this can happen even if no fundamental changes occur in the higher educational establishment; Karl Marx did not have to "liberate" the Reading Room of the British Museum to make it serve his purposes.

But the universities are only starting points. The world party will reach far beyond the campus, into civil services, businesses, the media, international agencies, all institutions and professions. It must in time attract sympathetic interest, financial support, and fresh personnel from those inside, as well as outside, the great centers of established power. Many younger men and women in such centers will understand with a special intimacy the hopelessness of the prevailing international system, and will be prepared to join the world party. Their adherence will be valuable in itself, and valuable also because revolutions rarely succeed until the *ancien régime* loses faith in itself, through the gradual decay of confidence among its own people.

It is also essential that the party evolve rapidly into a fully international movement. No one nation, or race, or traditional civilization has the moral authority or military power to impose a universal order on the rest of mankind. On the other hand, we must not expect anything like uniform growth in each part of the world. In some countries progress will be slow, perhaps negligible. In others—such as Canada, Sweden, Japan, India—we may hope for swift development, once a good start has been made. If the world party can strike deep roots in several countries scattered around the planet, countries where its position is more or less impregnable, we need not be unduly alarmed if it fails to catch hold for some time elsewhere. Local needs and conditions will force upon the party a unique plan of operations in every country.

The greatest differences will divide the national party organizations in the technologically advanced bourgeois democracies from those in the communist republics, with the parties of the underdeveloped noncommunist countries steering a course somewhere between the two extremes. Political realism will demand dissimilar strategies in each of the three groups of states, even at the risk of making worldwide cooperation among the national party leaderships quite difficult. If the party could limit its work to discussion among small groups of like-minded intellectuals, such differences of approach might not be necessary. But we must move whole populations, and our strategies must be attuned to local political realities.

The world party will initially find its greatest number of supporters in the bourgeois democracies, where disillusionment with nationalism runs deepest, and where private affluence and political liberalism enable many people to become active in dissident causes with little personal risk. But the relative stability of the bourgeois regimes, based on traditions and institutions that permit nonviolent change, and stifle political extremism, rules out any possibility of revolutionary transformations in the near future, so long as there is no major world war. Strategies involving violence must be rejected as counterproductive, at least for the time being.

In the bourgeois democracies, I would expect the world party to make its first appearance in a few large cities, as a coalition of exasperated liberals and radicals who can no longer function within the hopelessly compromised structures of the old leftist parties. The idea of a new world civilization may serve as the rallying cry of these liberals and radicals, but they will also represent the interests of oppressed or disadvantaged groups: racial and national minorities, youth, women, the urban poor, together with a variety of alienated intellectuals. As the party grows in size and wealth, it will be able to engage in an ever-broader program of activities, but it can devote itself from the first to what may be its most important task: public enlightenment.

I foresee a new insistent and messianic style of politics, serious-minded, yet joyful and passionate, a politics that never relents, a politics of peaceful protest, public festivals, and door-to-door canvassing, a politics that is, above all, visible and audible in the streets. Its posters and advertisements will appear everywhere. It will have speakers available for civic meetings, schools, clubs, wherever a platform is available. A very small party, if it has ideas and energy, can steal public attention away from the most venerable established parties. The tactics of such otherwise unrelated movements as the early twentieth-century suffragettes, the Yippies, and Jehovah's Witnesses will be studied and freely adapted.

In time, the world party will be able to put forward slates of candidates for local and national political office, directing special attention to the defeat, or at least embarrassment, of the candidates of the "official" Left. This may seem a somewhat cannibalistic strategy, but since the world party will rely for most of its electoral strength on leftist voters who nowadays reluctantly identify themselves with the official Left, no other strategy is feasible. By traducing the hopes for change of leftists everywhere, the official Left has in any case forfeited all claim upon our loyalties. It has sold out to the nation-state system and made its peace with capitalism. It deserves no sympathy, and no further support.

At the same time, the world party will endeavor to worm its way into the vitals of the established order, by infiltration of ministries and civil services, industrial concerns, churches and schools, the military, the media, wherever it can find safe *entrée*. Such infiltrators may be able to serve the old order loyally here and now. There will be no question of "treason" or "espionage" on behalf of foreign powers. But the men and women of the world party will use their positions within the system as centers from which to radiate new thinking and new values among the functionaries of the established order. They will attempt to shape policy. They will stand ready to take advantage of whatever opportunities arise, in time of crisis. They will be men and women of the new civilization, serving in the old, as Christians served late imperial Rome. As they serve, they will strive to convert their fellow workers to a future allegiance, an allegiance to a state and society that does not yet exist, but which every man helps to build by the quality of his hopes.

As soon as a generous measure of mass support has been won, it should be possible for the world party to launch campaigns of selective civil disobedience against the reactionary policies of the old order. The repertoire of techniques of nonviolent defiance of unjust laws already developed by organized labor, pacifist groups, and the movements for independence in India and for racial equality in the United States will be put to full use, and expanded, as the world party grows. Strikes, boycotts, refusal to accept conscription and taxation, peaceful occupation of public places, people's marches, unauthorized mass crossings of national frontiers, nonviolent harassment of officials and computers, and many other stratagems will dramatize the will of mankind for unity and peace. Such activities will jeopardize the positions of world party members who have permeated the established order, or reached elective office, and should not be attempted on a large scale until the earlier work of the party has aroused strong public sympathy. But their time will come.

Even in the bourgeois democracies, the world party must also eventually nerve itself to create a network of subterranean organizations prepared to join forces with party members inside the established order in the not inconceivable event that the ruling circles of the established order choose to abandon openly the liberal-democratic process and impose some sort of neofascist regime. The world party must be ready at such a moment to assume the powers of government itself, if necessary by force. It will not repeat the mistakes of the Italian and German socialists and bourgeois liberals who stood by helplessly while Mussolini and Hitler destroyed constitutional government in their countries after the First World War. Nor will it march unresistingly into gas chambers. Never again!

But the world does not consist exclusively of bourgeois democracies with advanced technologies and governments relatively tolerant of political dissent. Most of the world's peoples live under quite different regimes. If the world party confines its activities to the bourgeois democracies, it runs the risk of becoming little more than a movement for "Atlantic union," an instrument of the ambitions of a few wealthy nations who (except for Japan) speak more for Western civilization than for mankind.

The world party will at first face a much more difficult task outside the bourgeois democracies, but I am not sure whether the long-range prospects for success are any less. Perhaps they are better. On the one hand, most of the countries concerned are preoccupied, and may remain preoccupied indefinitely, with the achievement of national integration, economic well-being, and political stability, all of which the typical bourgeois democracy already enjoys. Their elites, it may be argued, are not likely to devote great amounts of time or thought to the problems of world integration until they have solved their most pressing domestic problems. Also, many governments outside the pale of bourgeois civilization forcibly suppress all forms of political dissent. The idea of an openly flourishing world party in countries such as China, the Soviet Union, Saudi Arabia, Spain, or either half of Vietnam is obviously ludicrous.

On the other hand, even if we make the unwarranted assumption that the bourgeois democracies will go on being affluent and stable for centuries to come, affluence and stability do not necessarily create the best climate for political movements advocating radical change. The world party will probably encounter less official persecution in the bourgeois democracies than elsewhere, but only because rich countries can better afford to risk dissent than unstable ones. It is notoriously difficult to persuade men and women with full larders to change their politics or their way of life, no matter how uncertain the future of all mankind may be. But in countries that have not yet achieved a high degree of national integration, in countries struggling to industrialize that cannot find the necessary capital, in countries confronted with imminent ecological catastrophe, in countries with despotic regimes that allow little or no participation in decision making by the people or their representatives, in countries with unstable constitutional systems, the world party may be able to make spectacular progress, if only it can manage to win a foothold in the national political life. In short, its program may appeal more strongly to peoples on the brink of total collapse than to peoples who still feel able to cope with their problems in traditional ways.

In the poor noncommunist countries of Asia, Africa, and Latin America, the strategy adopted by the world party will differ considerably from one country to another. In some, such as India, many of the same techniques employed in the affluent bourgeois democracies should work well. In others, the party will have to operate entirely from underground positions, while attempting to permeate ruling elites as best it can. It will strive to associate itself with the cause of the masses, as against bourgeois or feudal privilege, and against the remnants and residues of Western imperialism. It will argue the advantages to poor countries of a world economy in which gross disparities in wealth from one region to another are rapidly planned out of existence. It will preach the futility of national "solutions" to the basic ecological problems of contemporary mankind.

In a number of these countries, instability is so chronic that the world party will be able to mount successful political revolutions, and it will not shrink from doing so when its chance comes. In the 1970's, dozens of noncommunist nations in Asia, Africa, and Latin America lie in the grip of feudal regimes, reactionary military dictatorships, plutocracies allied to Western capitalism, or governments once radical that have grown fat and irresponsible in their middle age. By the time the world party becomes a prominent force on the political landscape—in ten, twenty, or thirty years —the situation in many individual countries will have changed considerably. But on the whole, we may expect that conditions will grow much worse than they are today. The need and opportunity for revolutionary action will increase, rather than diminish.

In the communist states, finally, the world party will have no choice but to go underground. Some contact can be maintained with the general population through the circulation of clandestine literature, meetings in private homes, and the like, but the greatest practical value of such activities will be to recruit men and women of outstanding abilities who can serve the party by infiltrating the ruling elites. Communist states are not invulnerable to subversion at the top. Factional struggles within the leadership have characterized the history of every communist state since the 1920's in Soviet Russia. If world party members can work their way up the ladder in communist party organizations, in the managerial class, and in the military, they will sooner or later have a chance to wrest power from the men who rule. Living a double life is always dangerous; as in other parts of the world, the world party may succeed in the communist states only in the af-

termath of some catastrophic domestic or international breakdown of normal existence. But the stakes are high enough to justify the risk.

Let us be sure of one thing. A world party cannot maintain its credibility
unless it operates throughout the world. If it flourishes in the bourgeois democracies, but not in the states of the communist camp, or vice versa, it
opens itself to the charge of playing Cold War politics. If it flourishes in
the Third World, but nowhere else, it cannot promise the cooperation of
the peoples of the bourgeois and communist nations in solving the vast
economic problems of the Third World. If it does not draw on the energies, values, aspirations, and knowledge of the peoples of all the existing
civilizations, if it cannot promise peace and disarmament for all nations, if
it does not generate a world will, it cannot create a world republic.

To this end, the world party must also appoint an international directorate drawn from the leadership in each country, with official headquarters
in a neutral state such as Sweden or Switzerland, and an informal floating
headquarters that might make most of the real decisions. In the early history of the world party, its directorate will play only a minor role, as a
clearing house of ideas, as a source of good counsel, but eventually it may
grow into a great political force in the world, helping to finance national
parties too weak to stand alone, and coordinating the activities of all the
national parties, weak or strong.

Concretely, the final goal of the world party in every country will be the
mundialization of national power, the transfer of sovereign power intact
and complete to the world republic, which can begin to exist in a formal
sense from the moment that the first nation-state accepts mundialization.
All the work of the party will be geared toward that end, although it will
involve itself in many other urgent national and planetary issues.

Yet, let us not build our hypothetical castles too high. My guess is that
long before the world party can overwhelm the nation-state system, perhaps before it mundializes a single country, a great war will erupt that al-
ters the world situation drastically. It might be an almost totally destructive cataclysm, for which we shall need the kind of "Doomsday insurance"
described in the next section. But a more likely war scenario is the "abor-
tively" total war, which causes serious loss of life and property in a few
countries, staggers the international system, modifies the balance of power,
and leaves most of mankind alive. In the wake of such a war, the conscience of the species will be badly bruised and unusually vulnerable to the
arguments of the world party and its leaders. If the world party then has

sufficient strength, it might seize power in one or more of the stricken com-
batant nations, taking advantage of temporary dislocations in normal political and economic life. But what matters most is that immediately after the
total destruction of mankind has been narrowly avoided, the world party
will be an already established force, prepared to offer the survivors an alternative better than waiting like stockyard cattle for another war to finish
the job.

Wars madden the warriors. In an age of total weaponry, wars threaten
all mankind. But they are also times when men are jolted out of the stupe-
fying routines of normal existence and challenged to rethink and restruc-
ture their lives. The first two world wars of the century helped to crush the
moral authority of the old civilizations and accelerated their inner decay.
The struggles since 1945 in North Africa and Southeast Asia have further
weakened them. Fear and anger are not enough in themselves to build a
new society. But perhaps only a third world war, with its risk of a literal
Doomsday, can provide the mental climate in which resistance to the logic
of world integration at last collapses.

In any event, it is clear that the world party will not be another institute,
foundation, or study center. It will not consist of a few earnest ideologues
vaguely supported by an invisible board of miscellaneous dignitaries; nor
will it be a registry or convention of self-proclaimed world citizens. It will
not be an *ad hoc* committee trying to solve one sharply delimited problem.
The world party of my vision is a political party advancing along a broad
front toward the realization of a world political order, in concert with far-
reaching movements in the general culture of humanity. It will meet with
fierce resistance in every country where it succeeds in establishing itself.
Sometimes it will have to act outside "the law."

But "the law" is only the positive law of the nation-state, whose willingness to resort to mass butchery in defense of "vital national interests" has
been demonstrated many times over in this century. The happiness and the
survival of mankind depend, absolutely and categorically, on the disman-
tling of these national structures. Such structures themselves now stand
outside the law: the higher law of mankind.

5. Doomsday Insurance

We must also try to cope with the dreary possibility that the nation-states,
in their pride and lawlessness, will make war to the limit of their powers.

One of the first things a prudent young husband (or liberated wife) does before raising a family or making his fortune, is to insure his life. Like the young husband or wife, modern civilization could expire at any moment. If our analysis in Chapter One is correct, its life expectancy is somewhat poorer than a present-day man's or woman's at age twenty-one. The existing civilized societies may blow up so completely that their passing will make the re-establishment of civilized life on earth impossible for centuries, perhaps forever. Some scientists argue that a total nuclear war with no holds barred would exterminate, directly or indirectly, all higher life forms on the planet. The fallout, they report, could not be prevented from eventually poisoning every latitude.

What sort of Doomsday insurance is possible for mankind? None whatever against world biospheric extermination, pending the colonization of other planets or the orbiting of permanent residential earth satellites. But for somewhat less ferocious catastrophes, policies can be written, and I suggest quite seriously that one fragment of the world revolutionary movement should detach itself from the main body at a very early stage and direct its energies toward the building of an ark of civilization, a renewal colony well enough staffed and supplied to guide the survivors of a total war back to civilized life and forward to human unity.

To judge from responses made to similar suggestions in the past, this idea will be dismissed by most readers as crankish and defeatist. Why not save it for an appendix, where it would cause the least embarrassment? or a footnote (preferably in Basque or Albanian)?

But I persist. No one is likely to be tied into a straitjacket for saying that the odds favor some kind of world military cataclysm in the relatively near future. The war or wars may demolish only a few cities, or kill only a few million persons—at least the first time around. We have already discussed the relevance of such abortive world wars to the cause of world revolution; they do not threaten civilization itself. But a wide range of possibilities exists between an abortive third world war and the total destruction of the biosphere. Many of these possibilities would leave enough human beings and enough resources on the surface of the planet to make the building of a postdiluvian world civilization entirely feasible.

If we can agree to this much, where is the difficulty? Few young husbands expect to die while they are still tolerably young, but they buy life insurance anyway, when they can least afford the premiums. Yet, when it comes to civilization, to the vessel of our social being, to the environment in which we find freedom and fulfillment beyond the grasp of any animal or savage, we do not want to hear about insurance, even though (for all we know) it might be our own children and all our blood descendants for all time who would inherit what our foresight contrived to salvage. Think! All this talk about holocausts and Armageddons is not simply metaphorical. They can happen. They probably will happen. In all sobriety, we must draw logical conclusions from sound assumptions.

The amount of Doomsday insurance now available is hardly worth mentioning. The major powers have underground retreats for some of their most strategic equipment and personnel, but such facilities will be prime targets for enemy action. Civil defense precautions are a bad joke, and private shelters are almost never adequately designed or furnished. Because of the time factor in modern total warfare, very few people could reach safety even if ample shelters existed. Any country that did spend the fantastic sums needed to provide a serious urban defense system might find itself the victim of a pre-emptive strike before its system was fully constructed, since a country many of whose civilians could survive a major war would enjoy a significant military advantage in any possible future conflict.

It must be admitted that modern states cannot protect their citizens. They manufacture weapons of mass destruction, the weapons are installed in efficient delivery vehicles, and the vehicles could all be triggered toward their destinations in less time than it takes to read this page. But populations are defenseless. The most practicable insurance against reversion to barbarism or further wars, in the aftermath of a third total world war, is the building of a renewal colony.

Let us imagine a war in which all but the worst happens. The combatants are wiped out, neutral countries suffer heavily from radioactive fallout and other side effects of total warfare. World trade comes to an end. The earth's population drops to fifty million, mostly located in the southern hemisphere. Technological levels fall back toward those of the early nineteenth century. After the well-organized environmental plunder of the twentieth century, the few raw materials accessible to a now rudimentary extractive technology cannot sustain recovery or progress. The world is, in any event, badly demoralized. Local dictatorships emerge and begin to quarrel among themselves. Civilization shreds away, little by little. One might invent a hundred other scenarios, and not one would be exactly right. Yet, the possibility of a steady downward spin toward barbarism, or of re-escalation to World War IV, is anything but remote.

A renewal colony in such circumstances could act as the representative of the conscience and mind of humanity, to inspire the survivors to pool their limited resources and found a world republic in which progress could resume on a new and more humane basis. If all civilization is lost in the war, and mankind is reduced to a few enclaves of savages, the renewal colony would itself become the world republic.

Our colony must be located in a remote area, and extensive research would be necessary to sift out the various possibilities. Most of its facilities would be established deep below the earth's surface—possibly on an island in the southern hemisphere, in Antarctica, in the Andes Mountains, in southern New Zealand; or in some Arctic location, in or near Iceland, Greenland, or northern Norway. An important consideration would be the political security of the colony from outside interference during the years before Doomsday. It might seek extraterritorial rights from the country claiming jurisdiction over the land it uses; it would no doubt require protection from piracy; a mutually satisfactory arrangement with a country such as New Zealand or Iceland should be possible—for a price.

The colony would consist of perhaps twenty-five hundred persons, including technicians in all fields, physicians, architects, geologists, journalists, psychologists, anthropologists, and specialists in management and public relations. It would have a particular need for men and women skilled in the arts of propaganda and persuasion, whose task it would be to link together the scattered fragments of postdiluvian humanity into a viable world order. For some colonists, an active and useful life before Doomsday would hardly be possible within the colonial community itself, and they would contract to live there for short terms only, two or three years. Other colonists might stay for longer periods, especially the research teams charged with planning renewal projects to respond to specific foreseeable world disasters. Margaret Mead has also pointed out the need for the development of a technology of ultraefficient cultural transmission to facilitate "the most rapid and thorough dissemination of the basic inventions of civilization on which the survivors of a world disaster would be able to build anew." The thirteenth chapter of her *Continuities in Cultural Evolution* (1964), let us add, is a well-reasoned refutation of the argument that civilization will automatically start up again in the aftermath of Armageddon.

The right colonial population is important, but the colony will need more than people. It must have a great microform library of the world's books, serials, works of art, and technical designs. It would also need a fleet of light aircraft for easy communication with the outside world, and if possible several submarines. Building such a colony and keeping its facilities and personnel up to date would involve an initial investment of, let us say, $200,000,000 and yearly expenditures of $40,000,000 thereafter—the cost of a medium-sized American state university. A few unusually farseeing members of the world's club of multimillionaires could make this their project, if they chose, and no government would have to contribute a penny. If the United Nations ever became more than a forum for diplomats, the colony could conceivably be financed by a special agency under its jurisdiction. Better still, the world revolutionary party might support the colony from its own revenues, although I very much doubt that the party could afford such a great outlay of money for many years to come.

Unfortunately, such a colony is needed now. To wait for the emergence of an affluent world revolutionary movement might be disastrous. On the other hand, colonists dependent on massive help from the established order might prove unable to liberate themselves from its values. One imagines them adopting the life style of characters in a novel by Ian Fleming, rather than the consciousness of authentic revolutionaries.

An alternative plan for Doomsday insurance, suggested to me by Ian Baldwin, Jr., escapes these criticisms. Baldwin envisages the growth of a world network of many small independent communities composed of scientists, artists, and other creative people linked by underground news media, committed to a simple life, located far from urban centers, and quietly engaged in the development of a new technical, aesthetic, and religious culture. Such communities would be largely self-sufficient, refusing involvement in the economic or political affairs of the old order. Although many would perish in a major war, others might survive, and help to rehabilitate and unify what is left of mankind in the aftermath of the holocaust. Since we need all the insurance we can get, I think Baldwin's ideas are very much worth pursuing. No one can be sure what kind of renewal colony would work best, under the many possible circumstances that might arise.

But without renewal colonies of some sort, we run the risk of losing everything. Nor should we overlook the psychological values of the new "colonialism." The very existence of thriving renewal colonies might finally persuade a good many otherwise able and imaginative people to extract their heads from the warm sand in which they are now firmly planted. The colonies would become powerful symbols, as well as instruments, of mankind's will to live in spite of the murderous folly of the nation-state system.

6. Utopography

As our renewal colonists burrow into their bleak Antarctic island, as our ideologues write manifestos of world integration, as our prophets create the rites and scriptures of a new world religion, and as our politicians campaign for office or plan *coups d'état,* everyone enlisted in the movement for a world civilization should also be giving relentless thought to the question of what kind of civilization he hopes to construct. Our work is not merely psychotherapeutic. Without its objectives, it has no moral right to exist. If its objectives are unclear, its right to exist is also unclear.

We must revive the utopographic tradition, which fell into disrepute early in the twentieth century. When modern man began to think that he lived in the worst of worlds, instead of the best, the writing of utopias seemed somehow frivolous. He turned to the writing of counterutopias, which showed how his worst of worlds would grow even more horrible, obeying the implacably evil genius of its inmost being.

Already, in the last few years, utopianism has begun to reawaken as a force in our spiritual life. Without warning, it has become possible once again to imagine ideal societies and ideal worlds, and to believe them somehow within reach. Rural and urban communes have sprung up, experimenting with new styles of collective living reminiscent of the utopian communities of the early nineteenth century. One can partake at least temporarily of utopia by spending a few days at any of several institutes devoted to new forms of group healing and personal "renewal and growth." Astrologers tell of a coming Aquarian age of peace and love. The New Left is saturated with utopian thought.

For some, the new utopianism is merely another form of despair, another way of expressing total disenchantment with the world of the bureaucratic-technocratic status quo. For others it is dangerously delusive, because it may build expectations that cannot be fulfilled, now or ever. If utopia means the perfect life, the satisfaction of all desires, it is an impossible thought: the desires even of one man are often mutually incompatible. To satisfy one desire is to frustrate another. Although we need revolutions from time to time, to replace outworn social structures, and although progress is possible along many lines of development, mankind cannot come nearer "perfection" than it is now, or ever was. Perfection is infinitely distant.

The value of the utopian impulse lies rather in its power to set men free from their apathetic or suffering acceptance of the world-as-it-is, and to give them self-transcending purposes. In this sense utopography becomes the picturing in detail of a preferred world; not a world that is necessarily perfect or ideal, but preferable to the present world, and consistent at the same time with one's definition of man. It may or may not be practically attainable in all respects, but it serves as a target for thought and action.

The movement for a world civilization must be an unending exercise in utopography. It must generate many utopias, and submit these rival visions to searching criticism. We may hope that all our visions will in due course freely coalesce into one, as the world will of mankind grows in strength and love. But for the moment, utopias are in short supply. We do not know where, as a species, we want to go. Why should we exhaust ourselves in forced marches, if no clear destination lies in view?

Even scholars can contribute to utopography. A leading philosopher of education, Theodore Brameld, has recently proposed the establishment on selected university campuses of "experimental centers for the creation of world civilization." Staffed by scholars from a broad spectrum of disciplines who are personally committed to the goal of a unified world order, such centers would attempt to translate their commitment into action-oriented, cross-disciplinary research. In effect much of their work would be utopographic: the planning of a new world.

Making utopography and the study of world order a major academic field is also the educational objective of the World Law Fund of New York, the sponsor of this book. Its most ambitious research effort to date is the World Order Models Project, designed by Saul Mendlovitz of Rutgers University, which has set up eight teams of scholars representing Latin America, North America, Western Europe, Africa, the Arab world, India, Japan, and the U.S.S.R., as well as a ninth, "transnational" team, each charged with the production of a model or image of its preferred world in the decade 1990. The completed models are scheduled for publication in two volumes in 1972. The World Law Fund has already published a four-volume collection of documents, *The Strategy of World Order,* edited by Mendlovitz and Richard Falk, used in many colleges and universities since its appearance in 1966.

Scholars will probably have less to do with the making of the new world civilization than they would like to believe. But they are trained to think. They view the world from perspectives inaccessible to most other men, which qualify them to practice the difficult art of utopography. In the remaining chapters of this book, a professional historian will attempt to design his own model of world order.

Part II

COSMOPOLIS

CHAPTER FOUR

Culture

1. The Mortality of Cultures

As we set about the work of envisioning a world civilization, we must define a few basic terms. Chapters Four, Five, and Six will discuss various aspects of the world "culture." Chapter Seven will describe the world "commonwealth." Throughout, we shall speak of a world "civilization." These are not interchangeable terms. By "world civilization," I mean the world society of the future viewed as a holistic system of values and institutions. Its "culture" is its substructure of values and value expressions, including religious faiths, philosophies, sciences, arts, folkways, and technics. Its "commonwealth" is its superstructure of political and economic institutions, which shape its social life. I can imagine no civilization without both culture and commonwealth. Each powerfully affects the other. Ideas from the cultural substructure support institutions and inspire institutional change. The politico-economic superstructure sets more or less clearly defined outer limits on the kinds of value options available to men and women in a given society. A ceaseless interaction occurs between the two.

Nonetheless, each can be studied separately, and our first concern will be to explore the culture of the coming world civilization. We do so with full consciousness of the mortality of cultures. The classical Mediterranean culture of the seventh to fourth centuries B.C., the Confucian culture of the Han Dynasty, and the medieval Western Christian culture of the eleventh to fifteenth centuries A.D. are all examples of organic cultural "super-systems" that underwent more or less gradual decline in succeeding centuries, experienced temporary revivals, and then disintegrated still further, reaching in time a point of spiritual asphyxiation.

The disintegration of a culture is always a traumatic experience for a civilization. The trauma caused by its failure is often fatal, although in the absence of external challenges, the society may continue to exist for hundreds of years without the support of a living culture. Such societies are very much like zombies: bodies without souls.

All the civilizations of modern man are in effect zombies. Their cultures have been disintegrating for centuries. Vigorous efforts toward renewal on new foundations, such as the Enlightenment in Western civilization and the Marxist revolutions in Russia and China, have not fully succeeded, despite socioeconomic and political achievements that will no doubt be carried over into the coming world civilization. The Enlightenment and Marxism suffer from the incompleteness of their revolutionary vision, and from an unhelpful negativism that has great destructive power, but only limited spiritual resources for the strenuous tasks of civilization building. Even if mankind were able overnight to replace the nation-state system with a world republic, uniting all the remnants of all the civilizations in a legal world order, such a republic would have no inner reason for being. Lacking a vital organic culture, it would soon crumble, or degenerate into a meaningless superbureaucratic hell.

Cultures, then, are no less mortal than states or whole civilizations. Only the unprecedented, but socially carcinogenic dynamism of a single aspect of Western culture, its technology, gives it a false semblance of life today. In all other ways, Western culture is breaking up rapidly, like a test plane flown at excessive speed. Some of the whirling fragments are fascinating in and of themselves, and there is no lack of creative genius in the various arts and scholarly disciplines, but the culture as a whole lacks unity and meaning. The Islamic, Hindu, Buddhist-Confucian, and Marxist cultures are in a similar plight, agitated but not revived to organic growth, by the same Western technics and by local sociopolitical reactions against Western world hegemony.

Cultural pluralists, as we noted in Chapter Two, argue that any world rule of law must strive to protect local cultures against encroachments from the outside world. Their model of world order requires the conservation of the present (fossilized) local cultures, and even many of the local socioeconomic and political institutions based upon them. But once we hinge our thinking on the assumption that cultures are not sacred and immortal entities, as much deserving of protection as human lives or mankind itself, other models of world order become imaginable. Recognizing the mortality of cultures liberates us from the desiccated formula of cultural pluralism and enables us to embrace a world-revolutionary doctrine of cultural monism.

2. Beyond Pluralism

The new world culture, in our model of world order, will begin to emerge in the closing years of the twentieth century; the ideological-religious-political movement for a world civilization introduced in Chapter Three may serve as its midwife. In any event, it will benefit from an unleashing of creative forces whose exact nature cannot even be guessed. It will also strive to orchestrate the viable elements of the old cultures. The plurality of cultures now in existence will disappear, and in its place will arise a great world cultural supersystem alive and flourishing on every continent.

The desirability of a unified world culture is unarguable. The common will needed to redistribute the world's wealth, conserve the planetary environment, abolish the system of sovereign nation-states, and institute a world rule of law will remain forever beyond reach without the development of a universal culture to which most men freely subscribe throughout the world. Clashing values and faiths, incompatible mores, and mutually incomprehensible modes of artistic expression undergird and perpetuate group conflict. The world culture cannot eliminate all forms of conflict among men, but it will minimize the possibility of violent group struggle by creating a universal identity transcending the solidarity of local groups. Paramount allegiance to the local group will be supplanted by loyalty to the pan-human group.

The arguments against a universal culture are anthropologically unsound. We hear, for example, that mankind must always be divided into rival segments because men will not cooperate with other men unless they have a common external enemy. Groups allegedly develop a common culture for the sake of maximum internal efficiency in the struggle against the enemy. The culture then preserves the group. Only—so this argument continues—if the human race were confronted with a great extraterrestrial foe, a Martian or Centaurian or Betelgeusean invasion, could it feel itself one, and create a world culture.

This is superficially plausible, until we question the initial pseudo-Darwinian premise that human groups form only to fight. In the presence of other groups or potential groups, fighting may be necessary, of course. It may even be quite tempting, since plunder is one of the most elementary methods of accumulating capital. But violent conflict is only incidental to the struggle for existence. The basic instinct of man is to eat, preserve and shelter himself, reproduce, protect his young, satisfy his need for love and companionship, and appease his curiosity. Communities form among those who trust one another sufficiently, who feel close enough in spirit, to work cooperatively toward these common ends. They are not simply alliances of convenience, contracted in fear or cold blood by incorrigible killers. The same intelligence and feeling of community that prompts men to associate in groups of a thousand or a hundred million can prompt them to associate in a "group" of three or four billion, if they come to believe that such a group can best promote the common welfare, and if the group shares enough values and life patterns to inspire mutual trust. There is no bar to the emergence of a sense of world community in the myth of mankind's instinctual need for violent struggle against external enemies.

We also hear that the existence of a plurality of cultures and communities is inevitable for "historical" reasons. Cultural differences arise because peoples are at one time relatively isolated from one another. Once launched along paths of separate development, they never undergo fundamental change unless compelled by conquerors or seduced by more highly civilized victims, and usually not even then. By this "historical" argument, the plurality of cultures is entirely natural and can be ended if at all only by ruthless imperialism.

Such an argument ignores the processes of cultural homogenization always at work within the *ecumene*, or zone of habitation. These processes may be accelerated, or even retarded by wars, but they are not dependent on violence. Within a given *ecumene*, once a civilization has progressed sufficiently to bring all its peoples into intercourse with each other, different local cultures and their values inevitably intersect and compete. Whether wholly peaceful or accompanied by warfare, such competition can result only in the triumph of some values over others. Lesser cultures may vanish entirely; others may cease to exist as separate entities, but will pass on fragments of themselves to the more successful cultures. In any event, peoples within the *ecumene* tend inexorably to become more and more alike. There are more differences among the ancient Indian tribes of

North America, with their populations of one and five thousand, or among the various island peoples of the South Pacific, than there are between New Yorkers and Texans, or between Irishmen and Austrians. The relative cultural homogeneity of the 700 million Chinese, or the 250 million Americans and Canadians, or the 300 million Western Europeans makes it quite clear that nature sets no limitations upon the size of a culture-sharing community, and that local variations tend to pass away as the scope of human intercourse expands.

The significance of these patterns of cultural evolution to the twentieth-century world is obvious. Because of Western technologies of transport and communication, the ecumene increasingly becomes the planet itself. We begin to live on the scale of the earth. As Teilhard de Chardin pointed out, the earth's sphericity at last takes full effect; all movements of thought, all ways of life, all values thrust outward in all directions, meet, interweave, and fuse. The flat world of endless expansive motion becomes the round world of endless infolding and integration. In the long run, we could not prevent a universal world culture from forming if we wished— except by wiping out civilization. The only question is whether it will come in time, and whether it will be a mechanical synthesis of the essentially dead cultures of the old civilizations, or a new organic system capable of further growth and expressive of living values. But to prevent cultures from deeply interpenetrating throughout the world is impossible. The mingling of cultures, writes Teilhard, "impels us towards the ultimate formation, above each personal element, of a common human soul. . . . Everything that rises, converges."

Of course interpenetration does not ensure that the world culture will be drawn equally from all the existing cultures. Many values of the new culture will themselves be new. Of older values, it is possible that far more than half will be Western, from the classical, Christian, and modern West. Already Western values, in science, technics, philosophy, art, and religion, and Western concepts of personal freedom, democracy, and social justice, have exerted a disproportionate influence upon the Eastern cultures. Only a Westerner pathologically fearful of the charge of "ethnocentrism" can blind himself to the fact of that influence, which has spread, as illustrated by the history of Japan since 1867, without any necessary assistance from overt Western imperialism.

At the same time, the West also bears full responsibility for the twentieth-century crisis in civilization. The present-day Western culture is the most dangerously unbalanced and cancerous on earth. If the coming world civilization is to keep its Western heritage safely reined, it must absorb vital elements of the traditional Eastern cultures. Eastern influence will prove especially powerful in the realm of ideas: in religion, philosophy, and psychology.

The deeper feeling for the unity of man and cosmos in Eastern thought, as reflected in Vedantic philosophy, Buddhism, and Confucianism, for example, may help to create a more integral relationship between human civilization and its cosmic environment than is possible through reliance on purely Western values. Eastern art and music will suggest new aesthetic pathways to the achievement of harmony between man and his world. Eastern techniques of direct perception and self-discipline will extend the boundaries of consciousness and the powers of mind. The titanism of modern Western culture, with its tendency to despiritualize communal life, will yield to the more organic wisdom of Asia and Africa, even if that wisdom fails to survive in any of its ritualized traditional forms.

Whatever the relative proportions of Eastern and Western influence, the world culture is easily defended against the old complaint that universal cultures are necessarily grey and uniform just because they are universal. Unity is not the same thing as uniformity, and the world culture should be several times richer, more various, and more interesting than any previous culture in history. It will incorporate elements from many cultures, displaying an articulated complexity of the highest order. Different parts of the world will still have different climates and topographies, and more economic specialization than ever before, with the formation of a true world economy. The world republic will also permit noncoercive and nonproselytizing minority cultures to maintain a separate communal existence, either locally or in worldwide diasporas, like that of the Jews. The leavening effect of such relatively closed communities on the world outside is well documented in history. Advances in technics, too, will help stimulate cultural change, although they will be subject to firmer public control than in modern states. But the world culture—if it is genuinely organic—will undergo ceaseless change even without the pressure of technical progress. All its supporting premises will act as the seed ideas of further growth.

The role of the individual human being in the new world civilization will also be decisive. Although in any culture the individual is the greatest potential source of diversity and the only agent of innovation, national communities have done everything possible in the past to force individuals to conform to approved stereotypes of personality. From the caste system of India to the "new Soviet man" and the "good American," the individual has been systematically depersonalized by the folkways of his culture. The more recent demands of mass-production technics and totalitarian politics only add new restrictions to others long in force.

As we suggested in Chapter Three, the world culture will not feel under the same compulsion as past cultures to exact total conformity from individuals. It will no longer need to regiment its populations for struggles against rival cultures and states. The solution of economic and ecological problems will liberate the disadvantaged strata of world society, who tempt rich nations and elites to institute repressive regimes. The collapse of values based on authoritarian claims to absolute truth and their replacement by consensual values, discussed later in this chapter, will in itself help to create a more relaxed and liberal atmosphere in the world community, an atmosphere in which private dissent is valued as a source of new insight, rather than merely tolerated as an unavoidable evil.

In such a world, the individual will be able to pursue his own truth, according to his unique temperament, personality, and abilities, and he will be free to draw on the whole heritage of man in shaping his life. Individuals will practice their skills and professions anywhere on earth, live where they choose, and conduct their personal affairs however they please. The existence of powerful technical means to detect and apprehend anyone actually guilty of criminally irresponsible behavior will make it possible for society to dispense with most of its irrational taboos, which in traditional cultures create a uniform life-style that inhibits not only crime but also deviance of any kind from convention. No doubt the majority of individuals will spontaneously model their lives after whatever becomes the new planetary "norm"; nonconformity in any society is a strenuous business, freely chosen by few. But to those who find the average or typical existence distasteful, other paths will lie open. Even for the conformists, life will be fuller than it is today in our warfare states with their passion for regimentation, their incurable Grundyism, and their self-justifying appeal to the authoritarian preachments of dead faiths.

3. Belief and Will

But how can a new culture evolve if our diagnosis in Chapter One is correct, if mankind has at least temporarily lost the power to believe, if scepticism and relativism have robbed us even of our confidence that we can know truth? Most models of world order avoid all mention of religion and philosophy. Both have become meaningless activities for thousands of intelligent people. They escape embarrassment by saying nothing, or dismiss the whole problem by relegating religion and philosophy to the domain of personal preference. The greatest questions in life become irrelevant. *Chacun à son goût.* Some like chocolate, others vanilla.

Certainly the roots from which cultures have developed in the past seem to exist no longer. Not only have the forms of belief and faith of the old cultures lost their validity, but many modern thinkers deny the possibility of belief and faith in any form. We reject divine revelation as a source of knowledge, or a summons to faith. The mystic's direct intuition of transcendence is reduced to "unverifiable" and "noncognitive" discourse. We deny that values of any kind can be derived from facts, and we deny that facts are truth. Value statements are verbalized acts of will, without cognitive content, and fact statements are fallible descriptions of appearances, valid only in terms of an arbitrarily adopted symbolic language and mode of verification. Neither God, nor intuition, nor natural law, nor the curve of evolution, nor anything else can tell us what is true, what we should believe, or what is absolute.

It is commonplace for angry critics of analytical philosophy and demythologizing theology to accuse modern thought of dodging the "real" problems, of becoming imprisoned in a sterile academic world of word games. But these critics cannot meet modern thought on common ground and offer convincing refutations of the propositions they deplore. Nor can they overthrow the equally "deplorable" discoveries of historians, anthropologists, and psychologists that all thought is relative to its age, to patterns of culture, and to personality.

Modern scepticism and relativism are perhaps the supreme achievements of the thought of Western civilization in its period of decline and disintegration. In a world where so much is doubtful, I cannot doubt the permanence of these achievements, unpalatable as they may seem to the humanitarian conscience. Scepticism and relativism are also supported by some of the deepest thought of India and the Far East, as expressed in several schools of Hindu and Buddhist philosophy, which from the first have avoided the brittle certainties of the Greek tradition, descended from Aristotle. Western man's confidence in his power to know the clear, indubitable, and unambiguous truth may help to account for the greater scientific progress of Western civilization—but that confidence is now, whatever else happens, extinct. One has only to study the fractured, absurdist, value-denying art, music, literature, and theater of modern Western civilization to appreciate how deeply scepticism has penetrated our souls. The artist, as always, reflects what he sees and feels; he is a faithful mirror of the mental and spiritual climate of his time.

Does all this mean that a new organic culture is impossible, or that cultural life in the future can consist only of value-free academic scholarship and technology? The end of religion and philosophy as culture-forming disciplines is not, after all, inconceivable; the end of culture itself, except as a bitter litany of negation on the one side and bland impersonal research on the other, is not inconceivable. A world without higher culture may not be a viable world in the long run, or a human world, but we must not expect the overthrow of scepticism and relativism by a counterrevolution of exuberant primitive faith. We must not expect the overthrow of scepticism and relativism at all. So far as we can tell, they are here to stay. We can create a new culture only by working our way around them, by finding bases for cultural life invulnerable to their attacks.

The fathers of the world culture will, I think, begin by accepting the analytical philosopher's separation of fact from value, and turn it to their advantage. They will abandon the attempt to know the good by knowing God, or nature, or evolution. But they will insist that knowledge—even tentative, fallible knowledge—of the perceived world supplies the valuing subject with indispensable insight into the conditions of his valuing. It tells him not what to choose, but what kinds of choices are available to him, with what probable consequences, under what circumstances. In short, our sciences describe the circumference of the circle within which rational beings can make rational choices. The more we know, although it cannot be absolute knowledge, the better equipped we are to render judgments of value and choose courses of action. The search for knowledge of the world is neither utterly fruitless nor utterly irrelevant to ethics and religion.

But the force that creates cultures, and has always created cultures, is the force of will. To know that nothing outside ourselves determines our values or gives the resolution to believe in their rightness, can be a liberating, rather than discouraging, perception. All that modern thought has demolished is the imagined sanction of acts of human will by an external will or by absolute knowledge of the nature of the universe. The will of mankind remains intact, no less than its physical strength or its intelligence. The will can recover from the shock of discovering the awfulness of its responsibility. It need not shrivel and die, however helplessly it seems locked in a comatose state today.

Relativity can also be enlisted in our defense. The judgments of value of a culture are relative to the historical and cultural milieu in which they are made, but this too has always been the case, and it guarantees that the options of the fathers of the coming world will not be purely arbitrary. At any single point in history, many thinkers in the spiritual-intellectual *avant-garde* of mankind may deliver quite similar judgments on the nature of the cosmos, the aspirations of mankind, the requirements of goodness, and the needs of civilization. Unanimity is unthinkable, but all we need are enough good minds to provide the premises of a new beginning. If the moments of such mental coalescence are likely to be rare in the chaos and despair of our age, nevertheless they can still occur. We are not mankind in the abstract, but men and women alive in the latter decades of the twentieth century: to us certain judgments will seem more cogent than others, just because we live at a particular point in time.

Clearly, the making of a new world culture lies within our power, whatever the obstacles. Man's instinctual value-forming faculties remain at his disposal. His existential situation narrows his options and forces him to act here and now. Bounded by knowledge, will can make the leap to decision. This is not to say that we shall be able to generate faith in anything we can imagine, no matter how bizarre, nor that we should abandon reason. But we can create a religion and ideology and morality of world order, a system of value commitment to the desirable and the possible in our own future, rooted honestly in the will to believe, our knowledge of man and cosmos, and the consensus of wise men.

This consensus of the wise, let us add, will replace the authority of sacred texts and churches. It is something quite new in human experience, and the culture it creates will be consensual, rather than authoritarian. The "wise" will have no power above and apart from other men. No one will be able to claim absolute knowledge or absolute righteousness. Tablets will not be brought down from the mountain, and individuals will be free to believe or disbelieve in the consensual wisdom, which in any case will change from century to century as the world culture unfolds and grows.

Does such a culture seem open to too many interpretations, a prey to all sorts of private whims and historical vicissitudes? Perhaps so. But our old dreams of the absolute were even more divisive. Every statement of the absolute invited the most fantastic feats of hairsplitting. No two interpreters of any absolute truth ever interpreted it the same way. Its very absoluteness irresistibly tempted thinkers to chip away at it, or find some way of changing it from within.

Does such a culture seem to float too freely in midspace, without anchorage or guarantee of its truth value? No doubt. But mankind must learn to live with uncertainty. It must abandon the superhuman ambitions of its adolescence and console itself with the deeper and more honest wisdom of maturity. Those earlier ambitions were quite likely necessary to mankind at one stage in its evolution. They gave us a certain daring and buoyancy which we may have needed to break through the endless cycles of primitivism. But now let us be men and women. We can still value. We still have hearts and wills. We can still search for the truth, never to be known in its fullness. We are still capable of faith, so long as we recognize its origins in our own wills.

And who can say? Although we seem to ourselves to float freely, perhaps after all we do not. In the words of immanentist theology, perhaps we are only the agents of the divine at work in the world; or in the Hindu formula, *tat tvam asi:* that thou art! We cannot know. Yet knowing is not all being.

4. The Service of Being

"Like many people," says the film director Federico Fellini, "I have no religion and I am just sitting in a small boat drifting with the tide. . . . Today we stand naked, defenseless, and more alone than at any time in history. We are waiting for something, perhaps another miracle, perhaps the Martians. Who knows?" Fellini's *confessio infidelitatis,* with its undertone of longing and anxiety, speaks eloquently to the spiritual condition of modern man.

But the "miracle" that Fellini awaits may well occur. The new universal religion glimpsed in Chapter Three will grow until it becomes the faith of most of the world's peoples. Although the world commonwealth will deny liberty of conscience to no man, it will resemble a theocracy more than it resembles the religionless state of modern times. It will draw back from modern impiety, from Western man's prideful refusal to bind himself to any form of religious discipline, and it will escape from the joyless vacuum into which liberalism has unintendingly plunged the modern spirit. As during the Reformation, liberty of conscience will become an opportunity for faith rather than a refuge for doubt.

Let us try now to imagine the world religion as it may exist by the middle of the next century, after the revolutionary Year One, when the world civilization has superseded the parochial civilizations of the past. We cannot penetrate very deeply into the substance of the world religion, because religions are born in the fire of spiritual vision, and the abstractions of ordinary prose or scholarship fall short of touching their inmost reality. But let us go as deeply as we can. If we cannot describe the religion itself, at least we may catch sight of its supporting philosophy.

The world religion must become, I would suggest, a religion of being, and the goal of its believers, the service of being. Other phrases also come to mind: a religion of personal fulfillment, a religion of mankind, a religion of the earth or the cosmos. But all these are subsumed in the service of being. The world religion will celebrate being. It will look upon the stuff of the world, the minerals, the fibers, the flesh, the life of mind and spirit, in their harmony, their conflict, and their evolution, and it will declare this worldly expression of being good. It will love the world, for what it has been and for what it will be. It will not accept the world, in the sense that it accepts any given situation as absolute, but it will intuit, without knowing, that the world is a holy place, that all being is ultimately one, and that the universe coheres. Not everything that happens in the world will be seen as good, taken in and of itself, but all good will be found in the world.

The world religion, if I am right, will distinguish three orders of being, each a complete holistic system serving as the ground of the next higher order, until the highest. The first is the cosmos, the universe as a formed and integrated whole. The cosmos is that out of which man exists, which includes man in its design for being. To human observers, this ultimate reality is like the root of a plant, and from its being rises the second order, the common stem of mankind. The prophets of the world religion may agree with the thought ventured speculatively at the end of the preceding section of this chapter, that in mankind the cosmos becomes capable of speech, intellection, judgment, and culture. Mankind is not alone in the cosmos: we grow from the cosmos, we have our being in its being, we were implicit in its earliest self-manifestations in space and time.

But mankind in turn culminates in the many flowers of its psychically and physically differentiated persons. Personhood may come to be seen as the third order of being. The person is not prior to mankind. Without mankind the individual human organism would still be a mindless beast; and only after thousands of years of societal evolution did the individual achieve true personhood. Injustice still excludes many millions of individuals throughout the world from fulfillment in this elementary sense. The person is the individual who has become a free moral agent, who is self-determined, who belongs to mankind, but chooses from his cultural heritage what he will believe and how he will live. He arrives at his own rule of life, founded upon but not dictated by the common life from which he grows.

The world religion will offer, as it were, a unified field theory of energy and spirit, a way of attuning each order of being to the others, and also of perfecting its internal unity. It will address the world as the mother and sustainer of mankind. It will address mankind as the form and reservoir of our common life. It will address the self as the highest and tenderest manifestation of eternal being. It will seek the psychic integration of personality with mankind and the universe; the social integration of mankind with its persons and its cosmic ground; and human understanding of the solidarity of the cosmos with its creatures.

Notice that each of these orders of being can be perceived existentially, and will, I think, be celebrated by the world faith in just this way. The prophets of the new religion will speak of the cosmos not as a construct of physics or metaphysics, but as the world we encounter, and of which we are composed. Similarly, they will see mankind not as an abstraction, but as the actual genetic material, cultural life, and historical experience that has created us all. They will see the person not as a unit in the mass of mankind, but as a living spiritual reality, a unique consciousness with memories, desires, and powers peculiar to its own being. In these three orders of being, all reality is contained. The service of God will become the service of this triune reality. Faith in God will become faith in the ultimate oneness of the triune reality, a faith which cannot be discovered by science or demonstrated by reason alone.

Many of the concepts of the traditional religions will be reinterpreted to express, at least by symbolism, the truths of the world religion, and may live on most vigorously in this form. The Chinese visions of the cosmic Way (*Tao*) and the will of Heaven point to the unity of mankind and cosmos. Indian thought dissolves the boundaries drawn by ordinary perception between the self and the ground of being, and discloses their inmost identity. The Christ who is simultaneously the mortal Palestinian carpenter, the messiah and prince of mankind, and the son of God, is a symbol in historical-existential terms of the bonds of love binding all three orders of reality. Each of the religions of the past has attempted to teach the unity of being, in its own way, and with its own emphases. The world faith will only perfect their work, in terms meaningful to postmodern man.

But of course it is hardly possible here to foresee exactly what form this consummation will take. New symbolic language may be discovered, to express in art and poetry the insights of the coming prophets. In Chapter Three we also anticipated the invention of new rites and spiritual exercises. Some of these may closely resemble the private meditative exercises of Indian religion, which develop self-discipline and deepen understanding of self and cosmos. The sacred dance, the chant, and the prayer still have possibilities. But I should not be surprised to find a gradual fusion of these traditional sacred arts with the arts of secular culture. The rituals of modern psychiatry, from the confession on the couch to group therapy; the concert of "serious" or "popular" music; the performance in the theater and the exhibition of painting or sculpture; and the (once sacred, but later desacralized) sexual orgy may all be transformed into religious celebrations. Man's creative energies will be reclaimed and reinvested with holiness by the new world religion.

5. World Morality

Religionless modern society is also a society without morality. It has no hope of goodness. The death of God, as Nietzsche wrote in his *Joyful Wisdom*, destroys our knowledge of good and evil. The recovery of the moral sense demands the creation of a new morality, founded on a new vision of man's relation to reality.

Nietzsche's own attempt to produce a new morality, his idea of the Superman, fused the aristocratic virtues of ancient Greece with the striving romanticism of Goethe. It was by no means a full philosophy of good and evil, yet it has a singing quality, a life of its own drawn from the strength of Nietzsche's personal will to power—or better, his will to self-mastery.

The most characteristic twentieth-century "new morality," the ethics of existentialism, makes of each man's life a project, and of each waking moment a fresh challenge to will. Translated into Christian terms, existential ethics asks all men to choose their course of action at every turn, guided only by the Christian doctrine of love. In either instance, there can be no moral "code," no list of commandments, no absolutes. The man who falls back upon rules and laws becomes the slave of cultural forces outside himself; he relinquishes his freedom to choose and act, and his life loses authenticity.

Both in Nietzsche's ethic of the Superman and in the ethical philosophy of existentialism, the new morality of the world civilization is foreshadowed. Neither is new in the sense that its substantive values—freedom, self-mastery, creativity—are new; their innovative power rests in their apprehension of the responsibility of the valuing self and the function of will in moral decision. If the world religion is to be a religion of will, so must the world morality be a morality of will.

Yet the will that values the good must accept the tutelage of religion. The best analogy is perhaps with modern Christian "situation ethics," adapted from existentialism, which makes personal decision subject to the all-encompassing demands of Christian love. Such demands are not crystallized in any creedal form, and the self still interprets and chooses; but it does so in the light of a traditional teaching that retains, for many Christians, its authenticity no matter what disasters have overtaken other aspects of Christian tradition.

For the world morality, as in existential ethics, the choices made by individuals must be made as acts of free will, and every situation will demand its own unique decision. No moral code will define good behavior in any concrete historical circumstance. At the same time, the service of being taught by the world religion will impose limits that its believers will freely accept, because they are believers. The service of being is itself, in the most basic way, a moral teaching, which argues that the highest good is the protection and fulfillment of being. Working out the implications of the imperative to serve being may become the principal task of world moral philosophy.

The encircling moral values of the new world culture, which must inspire and discipline the will, may be expressed in terms of three principles flowing from the imperative of service: affirmation, self-determination, and union; or—rendered in another idiom—piety, freedom, and love. Still better words could no doubt be found. Other guiding ideas may be needed. But without these three principles, a world morality is difficult to conceive.

The first is "affirmation." I have also termed it "piety," and I might have invoked Schweitzer's "reverence for life" and Nietzsche's "yea-saying." Could anything be more fundamental to morality? Is a new morality possi-

ble without the yea-saying spirit? A volitional morality confronts life, and
sees suffering, despair, greed, and conflict, and nevertheless affirms life; the
will knows the given world and knows it piously, as the son honors his father. Piety is not for good or unerring fathers alone: piety is for fathers in
their fatherhood. If we may agree that being manifests itself in three orders, as cosmos, mankind, and personhood, then the new world morality
will affirm each of these orders without exception, in filial reverence. Each
is our father. Each makes us possible. Each is prior to our will that acts
here and now.

The ethic of affirmation is an ethic that demands conservation and defense of reality. It makes suicide, murder, manslaughter, warfare, and ecocide crimes against being, which we commit at the peril of violating our
conscience as servants of being; although sometimes, as moralists have always recognized, the existential situation leaves us a choice only of crimes.
Yet no matter what we may do, in error or in necessity, the ethic of
affirmation recalls us to our primal duty of conserving and defending the
cosmos, the human race, and all selves, including our own. There is a profound difference between the man of piety and the man to whom piety is
alien, even when both men make the same practical decision in the same
situation. Their life courses will sooner or later veer off in opposite directions.

The second guiding principle of the possible world morality is "self-determination," or "freedom." Self-determination belongs essentially to the
thought world of Western civilization. As piety expresses an ancient and
universal perception of the duties of sons to fathers, so the ethic of freedom
expresses the modern Western perception of the duties of fathers to sons.
To believe in self-determination is to believe in the possibility of indefinite
progress, a possibility that only Western man has considered seriously, and
only since the seventeenth century. Belief in progress argues that the defense of being and the search for universal harmony are incomplete without an appreciation of the capacity of being for change, of becoming as the
time-bound mode of being, and of evolution as the process by which being
fulfills itself in the real world. When being is self-determined, when it has
the freedom to innovate, progressive change may occur, and perhaps in no
other way among sentient creatures.

Ancient thought, both Eastern and Western, could not encompass an
idea of progress because ancient civilizations were not affluent enough to
support a large population of free, self-determined individuals, and amelio-

rative change occurred too slowly to be perceived clearly as anything more than cyclical fluctuations in human affairs. Nor did it lie within the imaginative power of ancient science to develop a convincing theory of cosmic evolution. Unfortunately Western man's exaggerated confidence in his powers led to a confusion of the idea of progress with determinism, and in the nineteenth century Western thinkers often assumed that progress was inevitable, guaranteed by the "laws" of history or of evolution. A bitter reaction against deterministic doctrines of progress took place in the years immediately following the First World War.

But now that we have finally overcome the moral and intellectual fallacies of inevitabilism, progress is once again thinkable. The sudden public enthusiasm for theologies, philosophies, and ideologies of hope since the 1960's prefigures a new mental climate. The new hopefulness does not negate the despair of the first part of the century; it embraces despair manfully and looks beyond it, to possible better worlds. In this form, as disillusioned hope, as hope purged of hubris, the great Western belief in progress will be transmitted to the coming universal culture.

The principle of self-determination, like the principle of affirmation, applies to all three orders of being. Since only creatures with consciousness and the power of intelligent volition can be self-determined, at the level of the cosmos self-determination signifies the right of all intelligent species and organisms to fulfill in freedom the possibilities of cosmic being latent in themselves. On earth, freedom belongs to mankind alone; but millions of other worlds in the universe are most likely inhabited by species of intelligent life forms, and each shares the rights of *Homo sapiens*.

At the level of mankind itself, self-determination means the right of the human race to strive for its racial self-fulfillment, to make its own future democratically and freely, ruled not by tyrants or computers, but by the vital will of the living people. Self-determination for mankind means the right of mankind to progress.

The will of the people, unless we some day develop an intertelepathic collective mind, is in turn composed entirely of many millions of individual wills, whose freedom is the condition of mankind's self-determination and progress. Without autonomy, personhood is meaningless and futile. The man who has no free choice is the man stripped of personhood, the man who has become, in effect, a thing. Without freedom, he cannot even show love or piety, because no subjective will survives to choose any course of conduct at all: there is no "he." In this sense, as Charles Galton Darwin has written, man is properly a wild animal, rather than a domesticated one. His wildness is his freedom from subjection to other wills.

At the personal level, it follows that the principle of self-determination establishes the right to realize one's full potentialities as a human being, which demands of society that it make available to each of its members the heritage of the past, equality of status and opportunity, and autonomy throughout adult life. The principle of self-determination also requires that one person not use his freedom to destroy or curtail the freedom of other persons. One man's freedom is every other man's freedom. If self-determination results in the injury or enslavement of other selves, it becomes the dialectical opposite of self-determination.

In modern life, as in all past societies, freedom is often denied, and tyranny applauded, in the name of freedom. Nothing prevents a plutocrat or party boss from lawfully accumulating vast personal wealth, which he may use to curtail the free development of personhood in other men, while at the same time freedom of self-expression is lawfully denied to many persons whose religious, political, aesthetic, or moral values conflict in some way with the values of the prevailing culture. The freedoms constitutionally guaranteed to individuals in most twentieth-century societies are violated over and over again by public power in those societies, and many basic freedoms are not protected even by constitutional law.

The world republic will flourish in the mental atmosphere made possible by an authentically liberal ethical culture. It will protect, except when other persons are injured against their free will, the right of the person to freedom of belief, speech, publication, artistic expression, association, and assembly; to freedom of marriage, divorce, and sexual life; to the means of decent subsistence and ownership of personal property; to privacy, the control of reproduction, and the use of one's own body, including the right to die. We shall finally have done with the repressive authoritarian morality of the major cultures of the past, which was rooted in social needs that no longer exist, and which justified itself in terms of a supernaturalistic world-view that is dead in the hearts of most modern men.

But to serve being well, affirmation and self-determination are not enough. The conservation of being and its progressive improvement through the vigorous use of freedom demand one final guiding ethical principle: the principle of "union," which we may also define as "love" and the "will to agree." The orders of being do not exist separately. Each involves and requires the others for its own fulfillment. Yet each order, and each constituent entity of each order, is perpetually endangered by other entities and orders, in the struggle to survive and evolve. Only if the affirmation and self-determination of being are strengthened by the love of being, by the will to union with all being, can conflict be reduced to levels compatible with the continued existence and progress of being.

Love and freedom may seem to contradict one another, but in truth they are complementary principles. Without freedom, there can be no love, since only free entities have the power to love. He who is forced to love cannot love at all. But the free will to use one's freedom noncoercively, without curtailing the freedom of others, can exist only if one affirms and loves all other men. If we use our freedom noncoercively merely because we are forced by law to do so, then we are unfree ourselves. We can be free only if we freely love. We can serve being only if we freely will the harmonization of our private beings with the whole of being; the unity of being is the ultimate reason for our devotion to its service.

The will for union, harmony, and agreement may find practical expression in two ways. Men may seek the attunement of their wills to the universal being of mankind and to the cosmos itself, freely consecrating their lives to the loving service of being. They will also seek the greatest possible integration of being within each of its three orders. World ecological planning, for example, will represent an attempt within the limits of the possible to harmonize the mineral, vegetable, animal, and human kingdoms of earth—in short, to integrate cosmic being. The building of the world culture and the world commonwealth will promote the integration of mankind. Finally, men will recognize their moral obligation to achieve self-integration, health of body and mind and spirit, through piety and love inwardly (as well as outwardly) directed. Such self-love will not, however, degenerate into selfishness, if it is centered in a self that in turn remains consciously centered in all being. This is the peculiar genius of classical Indian psychology: it prescribes not only integration of the self, but also liberation from the self, whenever the self is misconceived as an isolated atom of spiritual substance and struggles, like Faust, to transcend its natural limits. Estrangement from being, as C. G. Jung showed, is the cause of all illnesses of the spirit.

Piety, freedom, and love are the modes of man's service of being, as I foresee the morality of the coming world culture. Only one question remains. We have referred several times in this and other chapters to the inescapability of conflict in human affairs—and just a few pages earlier to circumstances in which human choice is narrowed to a choice of crimes. I am not the first moralist to discover that man cannot always do good, even if he wills good. Evil may arise in many ways: when the good desires or needs of different orders or entities appear to be mutually exclusive at any given time; when the good desires or needs of the same order or entity are incompatible; when good acts produce unintended bad consequences; when no good choice is apparently available to the responsible agent; and when good will succumbs to evil will. Every act that would logically be described as evil in terms of the world morality outlined above has at some point in the history of mankind worked to good ends, intended by the agent or not. War, murder, and exploitation may be preferable in given circumstances to peace, heroic rescue, and liberation. Hence we can never be free as individuals or as a species from circumstances in which the prescriptions of morality are ambiguous or even inapplicable.

For all these cogent reasons, the fathers of the universal culture will be persuaded to supplement their system of moral principles with the humanizing wisdom of existentialism. They will argue that the good cannot be chosen for all time, but at every moment of decision must be freshly determined and chosen, in the light of available knowledge and broad principles of moral conduct. Only deliberate malice will be inexcusable, although even deliberate malice may serve good purposes in the economy of world history. World ethical culture can ask no more of us than our best effort to choose in piety, freedom, and love what appears in the foreseeably long term to be the greatest good, or the least evil. The absolutization of any course of conduct is both idolatrous and enslaving.

A culture consists of much more than a religion and a system of morality. The forms of artistic expression that may prevail in the world culture, I cannot venture even to guess. But in the next two chapters, we shall explore other aspects of that culture which are somewhat less inscrutable from the perspective of the 1970's: family and sexual life, and education and scholarship.

CHAPTER FIVE

Men and Women

1. Sex and Justice

The late Bishop James Pike was a virtuoso of the campus lecture circuit, and never did his young audiences feel greater rapport with him than when he caricatured in a quavery voice the ecclesiastical hack who seeks to solve all problems by solemnly invoking "the eterrrrnal moral law." Students of this generation appreciate far better than their elders the fluidity of morals, which are made (as Jesus would say) for man, and not as ends in themselves. Underlying moral principles change, although very slowly; the applications of those principles may change drastically in a single decade. The conservative, with his alleged love of history, fails to see that history, sooner or later, leaves nothing unaltered. No idea of the good is immune to time.

The ethical concepts developed in the preceding chapter are not entirely new, but they are also not identical with the thinking of moralists one hundred or one thousand years ago. They indicate the transformation and reorganization that the most basic moral principles of our old civilizations may undergo in the coming world society. When we reach the point of applying these principles in concrete life situations, I suspect that the differences between the old and new worlds will become even more obvious and more radical. In any event, a statement of principles with no attempt to show how they should be applied is almost worthless. Logically, many different societies might evolve from the principles enunciated in Chapter Four. The utopographer must exercise his imagination well enough that we can see with reasonable clarity just what kind of society he proposes for the future, and what, therefore, his philosophy of religion and morals means in the real world.

How will the competing or intersecting demands of different orders of reality be reconciled? What happens when freedom seems to prescribe one act, love a second, and piety a third, all different and all mutually incompatible? What becomes of the family, the schools, the economy, the state, the laws? How shall men live?

It would require a shelf of volumes to answer all the questions that need answering. But for the moment, let us look at a realm of life where change is likely to be quite far-reaching, and where change is already occurring at unprecedented velocities: the relations between men and women. All the great civilizations of mankind long ago established moral and legal codes governing sexual conduct, marriage, the family, and the status of women (as well as men) which differ only in detail from one continent to another. In each of these civilizations, as opposed to many primitive societies, the two sexes are assigned radically different social and domestic roles; women are treated as a subject race, ancillary to men; sexual behavior is severely circumscribed by a vast armory of prohibitions; and the relations between men, women, and children are reduced, from the societal point of view, to property relations.

The patriarchal society has proved until very recently impregnable to attack. It has been shaken, but not defeated, by Christian personalism, the medieval cult of romantic love, Eastern mysticism, the Enlightenment, and the entrance of women into the urban labor force. Its success through the millennia has been ascribed to human nature, to innate differences between the sexes, to timeless principles of order and decency; but none of these explanations explains anything. Clearly the patriarchal society is nothing more than the sexual dimension of the property system in all historic civilizations. Like many forms of racist exploitation, sexism (i.e., male supremacy) is a system of relations of production founded on private ownership. Sexual life, the family, and womankind have been regulated exploitatively in the interests of economic progress.

Such progress has worked incidentally to the advantage of the male sex; but together with slavery, serfdom, and proletarian wage slavery, the patriarchal society may have been indispensable to the growth of human wealth and the evolution of our urban technological societies during the past six thousand years. Despite its injustice, it may have been necessary. Despite its waste and exploitation and suffering, it provided—and perhaps was the only system of sexual relations that could have provided—the stability, incentives, and slave domestic labor needed to transform a primitive agrarian economy into the relatively affluent social orders of classical Rome or India or China, and the still more prosperous Western society of today. For a traditional civilized economy depends on much more than the productive labor of able-bodied men. It also requires the faithful services in the home (and the fields) of able-bodied women; it requires large numbers of children, who must be nursed and reared, and to whom property can be willed. For every male who has produced more wealth than the economic system allowed him to keep for his personal use, thereby creating surplus value, at least one female has been exploited in the same way. Upon the surplus value of her labor all of civilization has always relied, whether one argues that the principal exploiters of such value are the males in her family or the wealthier strata of society or civilization as a whole. Her life has been diminished to make the system of relations of production function more effectively.

But this involuntary sacrifice was never just; it is no longer necessary in many countries, and will nowhere be necessary or tolerable in the coming world civilization. Similarly, there is no justice in the savagely repressive policy of the historic civilizations toward sexual behavior, and no inevitability in their familial structures. As I interpret the ethical demands of the service of being, the world order of the future will ensure the equality of men and of women in every sense, not only under the law, but in the economy, in public affairs, in education, and in the home. It will liberate sexuality from all forms of social and legal repression, except to protect the unwilling from coercion. Unafraid of experiment and change, it will encourage the growth of a variety of new institutions for the raising of children. All these things are demanded by a fully matured morality of piety, freedom, and love. They can all happen in the world civilization with no loss of responsibility and no disruption of social equilibrium.

No doubt I have already evoked in some minds a kaleidoscopic vision of shrill viragos, Roman orgies, abandoned tear-stained children, a great tidal wave of filth and anarchy that will wash the world society into oblivion. Many poignant examples might be given of ruined men and women who rejected the wisdom of the past and found no better way. In an age of transition from one morality to another, obviously many will not be able to make the perilous crossing safely. Not only is it difficult to construct a new system of sexual relations, but we are haunted (like the first pagan converts to Christianity) by our old gods, our old senses of guilt. The "liberated" man or woman often discovers, too late, that he was not entirely ready for liberation.

But what of the thousands of millions of women throughout human history whose minds and spirits were stunted from childhood by a system of repression so thorough that most of them never understood what they had missed in life? What of the countless unhappy spouses, tyrannical fathers, emasculating mothers, socially manufactured sexual psychotics, exploited prostitutes, frustrated youths, frigid women, and puritanical maniacs who scream out to us from the pages of history and from everyday experience in the modern world? In their misery, they are no less pitiable than the dying soldiers on our battlefields or the serfs in our mines and plantations. They are the victims of an unjust order that rapidly approaches the end of its utility in human evolution. Let us try to foresee how justice can be done in sexual relations.

2. The End of the Patriarchal Society

Several years before the invention of the phrase "women's liberation," a young history professor at Wellesley College borrowed a vacant student carrel in the library to glance through a book from a nearby shelf. His eyes wandered from his book to graffiti scrawled on the carrel wall. One epigraph, in particular, held his attention:

> Study hard
> Get good grades
> Get your degree
> Get married
> Have three horrid kids
> Die, and be buried.

In the first three lines of the poem, the sex of the writer is impossible to guess. In the last three, it becomes impossible to mistake. For the first time since he joined the faculty of this venerable New England college for women, the fledgling historian made a raw encounter with feminine alienation. He had been teaching history as if the world really mattered, but the delightful young people who sat in his classes knew better. For them, the world came to an end at graduation. The true purpose of womankind, educated or not, was to bear and raise children in the fastness of the home. In short, the adult woman was not an end in herself, but a means to ends outside herself, a fact of female life delineated with horrifying simplicity in the Wellesley graffito. The history professor suddenly perceived that he was a fool, a player of academic charades, or worse, a merchant of mirages, who spent his life conjuring up pictures of a world that most of his students, in the nature of things, would never penetrate.

I know well how he felt, because I was the young professor. Like most members of my generation, I had been a more or less unconscious believer in Betty Friedan's "feminine mystique" or C. H. and Winifred M. Whiteley's "myth of womanliness." My wife was at home having many babies, my girl students were clearly more interested in the future careers of their Harvard boyfriends than in planning careers for themselves, and most of the young women I knew preferred breast-feeding, natural childbirth, and Doctor Spockism to competition in the labor market with their husbands.

Friedan's feminine mystique, in one form or another, is as old as civilization, and no doubt much older, depending on how much credence is given to the theory of an aboriginal matriarchal society. It arose with the assumption by the male sex of sovereign power in the family group, and the emergence of property rights. A man's wife or wives, together with his children, lands, tools, and other chattels, became his property. He required sexual fidelity of his womenfolk so that he could pass on his goods to sons of his own seed. In certain relatively primitive societies, he might loan his wife (or daughter or sister) to a guest, but this, too, sprang from his patriarchal prerogative. Religion, ethics, and the law combined to vest in the patriarch the majesty of sovereign power.

At the same time, a mystique grew up concerning women, to the effect that they were physically, mentally, morally, and spiritually weaker than men, fitted by nature only to bear and nurse children, maintain the home, and engage in various essential domestic arts or field work. Often they toiled longer and harder than their husbands, but always in a subordinate role, with little opportunity to travel, participate in government or business or religion, or receive whatever passed in the society for higher education. Every effort was made to secure for the male the fullest possible freedom of self-development, at the expense of the female. It is likely that in a purely communist and equalitarian society, no progress would have taken place at all. But the price paid by the second sex was very high.

What many women, and men like myself, have discovered in recent years is that women are still paying essentially the same price for essentially the same kind of "progress" in the twentieth century, even in such countries as the United States. The patriarchal society has proved more stubborn and powerful than feminists of both sexes anticipated at the beginning of the century. After most Western and some Eastern women had won the right to vote, to attend universities on a footing of equality with men, to work in the outside world, and to enter the major professions, feminine disillusionment and masculine reaction reversed the trend toward liberation as early as the 1930's. Women found men less than eager to welcome them into the world, and more than reluctant to help out in the home. Identity crises stemming from uncertainty about sexual roles became a common experience for adolescent girls and young women. The male backlash was swift and fierce. Although many women expressed a desire to become "New Women," there turned out to be only a meager supply of "New Men." The average male still wanted an essentially passive, dependent wife, who could nurse his ego, take care of his children, and supply him with slippers, steaks, and sex faithfully each evening. Voluntary renunciation of the pleasures of slave ownership is, after all, rare. Witness the American and Russian civil wars.

Not surprisingly, the "ideal" woman of the postwar era is not the vigorous New Woman of 1900, but rather the moronic blonde cow, all mouth, breasts, and hips, who poses no threat to masculine pride or power. Or, alternately, she is the East Asian girl encountered by the American soldier on his imperial missions abroad, praised in popular magazine articles as the "perfect" wife, because she serves her man selflessly, and never complains.

At the same time, what we might call the "masculine mystique" has been revived, heightening still further the contrast between men and women. Mythical supermales swagger confidently through adventure films and the pages of men's magazines, hairy and sinewy, yet sophisticated, accomplished world travelers and sportsmen, each a *sahib* whose subjects are women rather than dark-skinned natives. In cinematic terms, if Marilyn Monroe and Jayne Mansfield embodied the cow-woman, the archetype of the male is, of course, James Bond, as brought to the screen by Sean Connery.

Specialists in the social and behavioral sciences reinforce the feminine and masculine mystiques with reactionary "findings" that confirm the wisdom of the past and encourage women to renounce the world for a full-time career of womanhood. Books in this vein were legion in the 1940's and 1950's. More recently, the *Dædalus* symposium on "The Woman in America," published as a book in 1965, contains a number of articles by eminent scholars reemphasizing the deep-seated inequality of the sexes. Raphael Patai, introducing his *Women in the Modern World* (1967), argues that women have moved during the whole course of feminine history from traditional domesticity to emancipation back to domesticity again, though now on a voluntary basis. In the most advanced countries of the world, women are beginning to say, " 'Now that we have won the right to take an equal place in a man's world, we prefer to return to the home, to our own places in our women's world . . . , the role to which nature has predestined us.' " The women of Asia and Africa, Patai writes, must go through the same cycle, and when they have "seen the sometimes doubtful advantages of working with men . . . it can be anticipated that they will recognize, like their Euro-American sisters who preceded them on the same road, that the role which was women's throughout history by necessity is the one they prefer by choice. Then, and only then, will the process of the emancipation of women be truly completed."

The oligarchs of *Nineteen Eighty-Four* could not have said it better. Slavery is Freedom. Ignorance is Knowledge. Women are Animals.

But one need not peruse the chilling prophecies of a Raphael Patai to be convinced that the higher goals of the feminist revolution are still far from won and may, indeed, be less attainable than they were fifty years ago. Despite changes, the life pattern of females in the United States and most other Western countries has remained in the most essential respects quite close to the traditional model; and, of course, the life pattern of males has changed scarcely at all.

The female is sex-typed from infancy. "Feminine" characteristics are encouraged by doting parents. The little girl is expected to help with the housework. All around her she sees women performing women's "natural" duties, whereas men go out into the mysterious world and vanish from sight. Her toys, her clothes, the stories she reads in her primers, the ideas of the older children with whom she plays, all conspire to condition her for domesticity. She is given miniature kitchens while her brothers receive chemistry sets. The pop cult of romantic love hurls her into dating and face painting even before she begins to menstruate. "Irresistibly," Marya Mannes writes, "the American girl is formed in [the image of the house-

wife] from childhood, and by the time she is going steady at twelve her future is so clearly indicated that only exceptional will and courage can
change it."

Her fate may be sealed in grammar school, but it is only in higher education that the absurdity of her position becomes most obvious. Two-fifths of
the college students in Europe and America are women, but for most of
them college work is an empty ritual. The only practical reasons for attending college at all are to multiply one's chances of finding a suitable
husband and to lay aside a degree for a rainy day. Young men have no
doubt, Bruno Bettelheim notes, that their education is at least intended to
prepare them for a successful career. "But the girl is made to feel that she
must undergo precisely the same training only because she may need it if
she is a *failure*—an unfortunate who somehow cannot gain admission to
the haven of marriage and motherhood where she properly belongs. Surely
this is absurd."

So thoroughly has the young woman been persuaded of the merits of
motherhood and the disgrace of spinsterhood that she flings compulsively
into marriage in her very early twenties, if not sooner. In the United States,
more than half the female population has reached the marriage bed by the
twenty-first year. Then ensues what the whole world has decreed should
be the only really significant chapter in a woman's life. She has babies. The
"irresistible" promptings of "nature" convert what appears to have been a
purposeful human being with a mind and a spirit of her own into a temple
of procreation. For at least the next fifteen years she is expected to devote
all her youthful energy and intelligence to serving as the hub of the universe for several small, helpless creatures, while she in turn rotates obedi-
ently around her man, postponing indefinitely any plans she may have for
pursuing a vocational interest of her own. At forty she may return to work
or school, but for neither sex is it easy to start life over again in middle age.
It is especially hard for a woman, who has been conditioned since childhood to regard herself as little more than a peripatetic womb.

I have referred chiefly to the American experience so far, but we are discussing a world problem. The condition of women is far worse in most of
Asia, Africa, and Latin America, and in the southern part of Europe. Britain, France, and Germany follow the American pattern closely. Sweden,
Denmark, the Soviet Union, the East European people's democracies, and
China present a brighter picture, in the sense that women have been more
fully accepted into the working world, and their participation in the pro-

fessions is more than token. But even in such countries, men retain the commanding heights of power in all fields, and women continue to play their traditional role in the home.

Obviously, it is possible to argue that the great anatomical and physiological differences between men and women suit them for different tasks in life. Some scholars contend that women are more "instinctual," "earthbound," and "submissive" than men by nature. Women emerge as dark, mysterious beings, ruled by the flow of their bodily fluids, oozing blood and milk according to primordial rhythms over which they have no control. By the same token, men are "rationalistic," "aggressive," and "self-determined." The Rutgers anthropologist Lionel Tiger speculates that these differences between male and female temperament were fixed genetically by natural selection long before the arrival of civilization. In any event, all the antitheses conventionally brought forward to explain the psychological contrast between East and West, or between medievalism and modernity, or between the savage and civilized man, are enlisted to explain "femaleness" and "maleness."

But these antitheses, although not completely false, have been overworked. The anthropological evidence suggests that they can be applied more successfully to women in patriarchal societies than to women in other kinds of social orders, and therefore reflect nurture more than nature. "Women," as a New York psychiatrist recently pointed out, "don't need to be mothers any more than they need spaghetti." The exclusively maternal and housewifely role is thrust upon them by the patriarchal society, not by instinct.

Even if women were in certain vital respects very different from men by nature, these differences would not necessarily be irrepressible or fatal to feminine success. If men had not long ago learned to postpone, control, or sublimate their strongest sexual urges and inclinations to violence, civilization as we know it—bad as it is—would be quite impossible. Yet women are asked to surrender to their allegedly quintessential femininity without a thought, and deny every other dimension of their humanity.

No one has been able to measure the exact depth and width of the psychobiological chasm separating men from women. But we do know, beyond any doubt, that women have the same intellectual powers as men. Despite the waste of most of their highest talents throughout history, and the crippling effects of male sexism, women have made outstanding contributions in all fields of human endeavor. Where they are expected and permitted to equal men, as in opera, theater, and ballet, their professionalism needs no defense. But every woman is a complete human being, a person before and beyond her womanhood. She is entitled to as much fulfillment of her personhood as every man. If women are more neurotic, unstable, and unhappy than men, which I do not doubt; if they appear to be less self-confident, less boldly creative, less suited to positions of authority and command, which I do not doubt, the fault may lie not with women, but with the patriarchal society, which takes care to clip their wings before they are old enough to fly.

In the coming world civilization, only two solutions of the so-called woman problem are possible. If we accept Raphael Patai's definition of feminine freedom, we must restore the patriarchal society in all its rigor. Rather than prolong woman's agony, we shall prohibit female employment and deny all girls admission to high schools and universities. Let them learn the domestic arts at home or in wooded retreats. Common humanity will also require that prefrontal lobotomies be performed on every girl before she reaches the age of five. We shall abolish female suffrage, following the example set by Mussolini in 1928. A system of *purdah* will be universally adopted. Women will be spared the bitter frustrations that always attend the enlightenment of the unfree when enlightenment is not promptly followed by emancipation.

But if we choose to continue the education of women, if we choose to give them any access to the world outside the home, then we must go all the way. The patriarchal society must be obliterated, by schooling, by anti-sexist evangelism, and by law. I cannot doubt that this is the course which the world civilization will pursue. The end of patriarchism will mean nothing less than the acceptance, as Alice S. Rossi suggests, of "a socially androgynous conception of the roles of men and women." Men will assume an equal responsibility with women in the home; women will be expected to share fully in the work of the outside world.

Much depends, of course, on what sort of family structures will flourish in the world civilization, and how work will be organized. I foresee extensive changes in both spheres, which must be discussed later. But for the present, it is enough to note that equality of participation can be achieved only by a thoroughgoing revolution in attitudes and mores. No existing civilized society has reached even the halfway point in this revolution. In a sexually equalitarian social order, fathers will spend as much time rearing children as mothers. Household tasks will be shared as a matter of course, from the preparation of meals to the washing of clothes. Some division of labor may occur, but according to personal preference and not according to any predetermined sexual role. Most important, each spouse will find employment in the outside world up to the limits of his ability, desire, and need. Sexual discrimination will disappear, and each adult human being regardless of sex or marital status will engage in work that best fulfills the requirements of his personal condition.

The end of the patriarchal society entails a complete restructuring of attitudes toward work, and above all women's work. A person's vocation in a society that has passed beyond the employment of human beings as mere instruments for the production of national wealth, must be a vocation that helps bring to full development his personhood. In the patriarchal society, such fulfillment is usually possible only for men, when it is possible at all. When women work, it is almost invariably in the less prestigious jobs, for lower wages, at the pleasure and convenience of their husbands; they are the odds and ends of any modern national labor force. But in the great society of the future, women will choose their vocations with as much care and forethought as men. Every woman—to the same degree as every man—will have a life's work, and will rise as far in her chosen field of endeavor as her abilities warrant. We catch the most convincing glimpses of this future equality, as noted above, in the careers of professional actresses and prima donnas, who command the same respect and rewards as their male counterparts.

Parents will also avoid discriminatory treatment of their children on the basis of sex. Girls will not be raised primarily as breeding stock. The conventional sheltered girlhood of the past will one day seem as ridiculous and inhumane as a harem. Girls will receive vocational training and higher education in the same proportion as boys, and there will be no thought of automatically depriving a sister for the sake of her brother.

I think the results of authentic sexual equality will astonish us. Women today, although legally emancipated in many countries, are not much freer than the black freedmen of the late nineteenth century in the American Deep South. They suffer from inferiority complexes, from role confusion, and from an ancient heritage of exploitation. The patriarchal culture too often renders them insipid and insecure. But the independent woman of the future will be very different from her modern ancestress. She will be a more exciting sexual companion, a more stimulating mother, a more professional colleague, and a happier human being. In the long run, men will profit from the feminist revolution as much as women. The world around them will be richer, and their own personalities will be liberated from the dulling effects of self-indulgent sexist despotism. In learning to treat women as ends rather than means, they will further their own humanization.

Of course we must not imagine that the sexes will become absolutely indistinguishable in the world civilization. It is always possible that significant differences in temperament do exist, bred into the genes and chromosomes by a million years of evolution. The impact of such differences may be largely nullified by other factors, both biological and cultural, but it could remain strong enough to prompt one sex to choose certain kinds of work, for example, more often than the other sex, even in the most equalitarian social order. If such things happen, freely and spontaneously, so be it. Also, the dynamics of heterosexual loveplay will continue to favor differences in dress and manners. The cow-woman and the ape-man become subhuman only when the celebration of their sexuality results in the suppression of their personhood. In themselves, the features that distinguish the sexes are beautiful; they should be cultivated with joy.

Nor should women's liberationists indulge in fantasies about world salvation through victory over sexism. The full liberation of women in the civilizations of the present age would not delay by one year the time of their inevitable collapse. If all else remained unchanged, freeing women to share equally in the sorrows of our moribund societies might conceivably do nothing more than add to the sum of human suffering. But female liberation will be one of the greatest tasks of the coming world civilization. Men who think of this as a peripheral or even humorous issue cannot be reminded too often: we are discussing the happiness of half the human race.

3. The Liberation of Eros

Intimately linked to the repression of women by the patriarchal society is its repression of Eros. To safeguard the family, preserve rights of property and inheritance, and discourage eroticism, patriarchal ethics limit sexual experience to heterosexual intercourse between legally married persons. There is also a reluctant tolerance of pre- and extramarital intercourse between men and female sex serfs (prostitutes), who provide sexual variety for men without running the risk of adulterating the paternal line; and until recently, tolerance of discreet pre- and extramarital affairs between men of "higher" classes and races and women of "lower" classes and races, which avoids the same risk and provides the same gratification for the dominant sex.

But any kind of sexual activity before or outside marriage is officially disapproved, and even sexual activity within marriage is permitted by most patriarchal societies only as a concession to human frailty. So much older and more widespread than Reformation Puritanism, the "puritan" tradition condemns sexual relations and the genital organs as filthy *per se*. This attitude is nowhere more vividly expressed than in the Anglo-Saxon definition of literary and pictorial matter related to sex as "smut." Most "smut" does nothing more than describe or depict men and women engaged in genital lovemaking. Often the persons involved may be married or represented as married. But this makes no difference. A picture of a woman fucking with a man is filthy *per se*, and so is my use of the verb "fuck," which for many centuries has been the most common word to denote sexual intercourse in the English language.

The psychic mutilation that results from the patriarchal attitude toward sexual activity is almost measureless. The leading school of modern psychiatric thought, the school of Sigmund Freud, has constructed a complete theory of human nature from clinical observations of the effects on the mind of the erotic impulses and their repression by society. The theory perhaps claims too much. But Freud revealed more fully than ever before the depths of the suffering to which the traditional sexual ethic condemns *Homo sapiens*.

Let us not cut our words too fine. The patriarchal society has chained up erotic life with bonds of guilt, embarrassment, and taboo. It has made both sexes ashamed of their desires. It has driven men to treat women as vessels of filth who soil whatever they touch. It has created millions of erotically frigid and frustrated women. It has attempted with some success to prohibit masturbation, contraception, abortion, group sex, and heterosexual "sodomy." It has legislated against all innovations in forms of marriage and fought a vicious war against the right of divorce. It has sought to deny sexual enlightenment and experience to young people. It has denied writers and artists freedom of expression. It has persecuted with unrelenting fury the one man or woman in twenty whose erotic feelings are exclusively homosexual. The survival of strong sexual feeling through all the long eras of puritanical despotism is a triumph of nature over human fear and malice. Or let us say once again, a triumph over a necessary historic evil.

Most of the sexual repressiveness of patriarchal society was perhaps essential to its economic progress. Capital accumulation was facilitated, or men had reason to think it was facilitated, by sexual sacrifice, especially on the part of women. In the agricultural and early industrial ages, antieroticism created a society in which stable nuclear families could be more easily maintained and the property rights of men in their wives and children could be more efficiently guarded. Energies that might have been spent on sexual activity were saved for productive work. At least, a rational apologist for the patriarchal sexual ethic could so argue.

But the world has changed. Reliable techniques of contraception and abortion remove the danger of children being born who are not wanted or will not be properly reared. In any case, the demographic predicament of mankind requires a sharp curtailment of the birth rate, shrinking the old taboos against contraception and sexual "deviation" to nonsense. Nor will women tolerate much longer their past status as the sheltered property of men. Female autonomy and the patriarchal sex ethic are mutually exclusive. They cannot exist together on the same planet. With most of the practical justification for patriarchism extinct, life comes fully under the authority of the same ethical principles that may regulate the rest of life in the world culture: piety, freedom, and love.

At the present stage of mankind's evolution, the principle of piety in the sexual realm prescribes not only the ecological sanity of zero population growth, but also the final dissolution of the moral nexus between sexuality and reproduction. In his sexual life, man in the world civilization will no longer be primarily the progenitor, the machine for reproduction, but a child of being who expresses the fullness of being in all his life, including the life of Eros. He will manifest his reverence for being by his whole life expression, rather than by obeying the merely animal imperative to multiply. Life, including erotic love, will be for itself. At the same time, piety will forbid any form of Eros that involves the injury or coercion of other human beings. It must be a conserving, not destroying, sexuality.

Our second principle, the principle of freedom, compels the liberation of Eros from the shackles of irrational taboo. With Erós no longer arbitrarily confined to reproduction or marriage, many once forbidden modes of erotic self-expression become legitimate. Pure sexuality is after all only a form of play, the kind of creative and fulfilling play out of which all human achievement flows. The time "lost" in pursuing or making love is time later regained with interest, because of the quickening power of erotic experience.

The liberation of Eros in the coming world culture means quite simply unlimited freedom of noncoercive sexual experience. Men and women will form whatever liaisons they like. Such liaisons will develop as easily and openly as nonsexual friendships develop today. They may or may not lead to marriage and children. They may last for many years, or only a week, just as nonsexual relationships do now. At times these liaisons may result in a deep sharing or fusing of personal being, and at other times they may be almost impersonal, each partner protecting his inner self against intrusion. As Harvey Cox writes in *The Secular City,* there is a place in human life for "I-you" as well as "I-thou" relations, for impersonality as well as intimate commingling. To the mind impregnated with the romantic doctrine of "one love, deep and forever," such ideas may seem immoral. But the romantic doctrine is in many respects only a way of reinforcing or sugar-coating patriarchical sexual possessiveness. By denying the richness and variety of erotic life, it seeks to render more bearable the male's absolute possession of his wife.

Thus we can expect in the coming culture a glad acceptance of group or orgiastic sex, of homosexuality and bisexuality, of explicitly erotic art and literature, of the consenting enactment of sadomasochistic fantasies (which can be just as therapeutic as reading "escapist" fiction), and of voluntary prostitution by either sex. Prostitution, of course, is usually an exploitative and degrading form of work in the patriarchal society. But in an erotically liberated society, the professional prostitute—freed of the danger of being cheated or coerced by pimps and gangsters—will become a respected citizen. The professional prostitute will not be drawn from the ranks of a depressed proletariat, if only because our socialist commonwealth (sketched in Chapter Seven below) will not allow a depressed proletariat to arise. He or she will enter the profession voluntarily, because he or she finds it interesting, and the standing of prostitutes in society will be similar to that of professional golfers, hair stylists, nightclub entertainers, physical therapists, or fashion models in the present-day world. On the other hand, it is also conceivable that we shall all become such good amateurs in the business of erotic love that no market for professional services will exist!

In a free society, many more people will have many more kinds of erotic experiences than they enjoy today. Herbert Marcuse in *Eros and Civiliza-*

tion anticipates the cultivation of a "polymorphous perversity" that suggests very much what I have in mind. A great deal of latent homosexuality, for example, will come out of hiding and many individuals will find themselves able to enjoy sexual relations with their own as well as the opposite sex. The myth that the unusual is automatically perverse and the perverse is automatically sick will be buried once and for all. Some unusual behavior, to be sure, is socially indefensible and quite psychotic. But in the life of Eros, as in all other realms of life, experiment and diversity can be entirely wholesome, if only the taboos invented by the witch doctors of puritanism are laughed away. A single smile sometimes demolishes them.

But there must be a third principle at work in the free society of the world civilization: the principle of love. If freedom of self-expression of erotic desires is not to lead to a self-destroying selfishness, it must be enriched with the power of love. Even a casual and relatively impersonal sexual liaison needs a little of this power to preserve its human quality. The sneak-and-grab promiscuity of traditional "immorality" must be replaced by sexual generosity, a spirit of give and let give, from which exploitation, possessiveness, jealousy, and niggardliness are all excluded. One need not always "fall in love," but he must love the humanity and the cosmic being in his fellow men. The erotic impulse is, at bottom, an impulse to love, to fuse, to seek union—however briefly—with being. When it is diverted into pure self-seeking, as in the traditional patriarchal marriage "contract," it is prostituted more completely than any girl in a brothel. When it becomes an excuse for jealous rage and violence, it loses all meaning.

We may even expect the rise of what Lars Ullerstam has called "sexual Samaritanism," a new class of volunteer social workers who love mankind well enough to provide sexual services for those least able to negotiate sexual liaisons by themselves, such as the aged, the insane, the crippled, and the very shy, whose desires may be great, but who are condemned to perpetual chastity by a society that fears and denies Eros. Sexual Samaritanism is a perfectly natural application of the principle of love to human need.

Indeed, the free society of the future will go far beyond erotic liberation to achieve full sensual liberation, the right of all persons to enjoyment of all their senses. Puritanism has always tended to look on every kind of sensual gratification as evil. Puritans object to everything—dancing, visual art, music, poetry, the theater, all stimulants, whatever brings joy and beauty into life. True, one can become so intoxicated sensually that he loses his equilibrium and his freedom; but men must be free to take such risks. The total development of human potentiality for mastery and understanding of the world requires that we exploit to the full our capacity for experience, not only through the mind and spirit, but also through the ear, the eye, the senses of smell and of taste and of touch, in which—in any event—mind and spirit also share. A bottle of wine, a well-cooked meal, a gallery of paintings, a festival of music, or an evening of marijuana may belong as much to the complete life as a book of philosophy, a religious ceremony, or a love affair.

But some readers may wonder how a historian, of all people, can so completely ignore the "lessons of history." Inevitably our vision of an erotic or sensual world culture must call to mind the popular legend of the fall of Rome. Are we picturing the end of an age, rather than the model of a new world? Didn't *la dolce vita* cause the downfall of the great Roman state?

Historians are still divided on the question of the causes of Roman degeneration and collapse—or the fall of any great empire in world history. The first point to make is that Rome was a pacifying and often civilizing imperial power for more than six hundred years; by comparison the Pax Britannica, or Americana, or Sovietica are mere mushrooms, quick to grow and quicker to die. But quite apart from the question of longevity, we must appreciate that only a handful of Romans enjoyed the sweet life satirized by Juvenal and Martial. The sybaritic pleasures of the elite were taken at the expense of the masses, and what finally destroyed Rome was not debauchery but public poverty, economic depression, the stagnation of thought and enterprise, the absence of democratic institutions—in short, the failure of the old republican system to grow up to the full responsibilities of imperial rule, despite many signal achievements in law and public works. Not Eros, but mindless conservatism and corrupting extremes of wealth and poverty are the true scourges of empires.

In any event, Romans did not waste all their substance in orgies. The poets exaggerate, and in so doing they reveal how much the Roman mind remained a captive of the patriarchal morality. When Eros is fully liberated, in thought as well as in action, men and women may actually devote less time to the pursuit of sexual pleasure than they do now. When sex takes its natural place alongside other human activities, when it ceases to be forbidden fruit, a source of endless frustration and shame, we may look forward to a society where sexual extremism is no greater a problem than gluttony, and morbid obsession with sexual themes is less common than in the various patriarchal societies.

4. Families

John Stuart Mill once called the patriarchal family "a school of tyranny." So it is. Conservative opinion insists on the sacrosanctity of the family, as the strongest redoubt of its moral system. Giving women equality with men outside the home, or relaxing the taboos against erotic love may not be fatal to patriarchism if its form of the family remains intact. The patriarchal family protects its members against feminism and free love, whatever changes occur elsewhere in the society. The family is a school of tyranny, and also of property lust, narcissism, and the most ferocious kinds of interpersonal struggle known to mankind. But the patriarchal society is inconceivable without it. The free society of the future must develop alternative structures of common life.

The tyrannous character of the patriarchal family stems from the traditional role of the father as owner and master of his children and wife (or of his wives, in the polygynous variant of patriarchal family organization). The family revolves around its lord: it becomes a living extension of his will. When the paterfamilias works to increase the family fortune, he is working for himself. When he decks out his wife in splendid clothes and sires many sons and leaves them great wealth, he is enlarging himself. What began as compensation to the Stone Age hunter for having to share his meat with womenfolk and their offspring, has grown into power far beyond the reach of any hunter's imagination.

In the most highly advanced patriarchal societies, the mother typically has shed some of her servility and enjoys modest rights within the home, but she adopts the mental outlook of her husband to a very large extent, and the family remains an inward-turning, conservative, and acquisitive social unit; a hothouse where all legitimate sexual life must be lived, where all children must be raised, and where all property must be hoarded. The patriarchal family reaches its apogee of absurdity in the modern Western suburban nuclear family unit, the most drastically involuted familial structure of all, consisting of one man, one woman, and three or four children, living in a box (house) or cell (flat), constrained to eat and sleep together, entertain one another, and spend nearly all their free time together, three hundred and sixty-five days a year, enjoying only the most perfunctory and superficial contact with neighbors, business associates, and relatives. As divorce becomes steadily easier to obtain, more and more of these families, exhausted by relentless intimacy, shatter under the strain.

But modern technocracy seems to leave these Westerners no choice. It dissolves the old organic community life of the past and converts its citizens into free-floating depersonalized fragments who can find no other social institution to fall back upon for the pleasures of intimacy except the nuclear family. Certainly one cannot be intimate with one's rivals in the labor market, or the people who—for the moment—happen to live next door. As for cousins and uncles and grandparents, they are scattered in various parts of the world in boxes and cells of their own, often inaccessibly remote. The nuclear family is the only hole in which to hide.

Men and women form such family units at a very early age in the contemporary Western world. The age of first beginnings drops every decade. Many "men" and "women" marry in their middle or late teens, victims of the steamy romanticism merchandised by all the mass media. If they do not actually marry, they engage in "steady dating" or live together, which often leads to marriage, and in any event amounts to the same thing.

At first all is well. But too often romantic love fades and dies. The "I-thou" nexus of authentic encounter deteriorates into the "I-it" relationship of the masculine and feminine mystiques. The man sees his wife as a cook, housekeeper, nursemaid, and private whore. She is a means to his ends; she has her life in and through him. At the same time, the wife gradually ceases to think of her husband as another human being. The ruthless possessiveness of the male is avenged by the development of a parallel possessiveness in the female. According to a recent survey, the average American housewife views her husband as a breadwinner first, a father for her children second, and a husband and lover last. She becomes estranged from him psychically, understanding little of his work, seeing him as a mere object, a means to her ends as the house queen. She realizes that she is nothing in the eyes of the masculine world, but in her own little kingdom of children and appliances, she is the sole potentate.

Some of these ills can be overcome when men accept women as full-fledged persons in their own right, and women are no longer condemned to a lifetime of menial household labor. But the modern nuclear family would often fail even in a sexually equalitarian society, for the simple reason that it is asked to carry burdens greater than any two people alone can bear. It is also a moral failure: I cannot imagine a structure better designed to promote irreverence for the being of mankind and the cosmos. Even if it permits the development of personality, it remains—to paraphrase Mill—a perfect school of possessiveness, both sexual and material.

The larger or "extended" family of the non-Western and Latin worlds, which brings grandparents, grandchildren, aunts, uncles, and cousins into close association with the members of the nuclear family, escapes some of the worst shortcomings of the nuclear family bond; but it fosters authoritarianism and social introversion just as strongly. It is also a purely arbitrary grouping, founded on the accidents of kinship rather than choice. For this reason it fares poorly in societies that place a high value on personal freedom.

In the coming world culture, there will be families, but I anticipate a great variety of familial structures, formed for many different purposes. The freedom of choice of mates insisted upon by modern young people will be enlarged to include freedom of choice of family organization. Every family will serve man's need for intimacy, but otherwise I foresee no common denominator—erotic, reproductive, economic, or cultural.

The basic unit of patriarchal family life, the pair bond of man and wife reinforced by law, is perhaps the only type of marital contract that will disappear in the new world. A man and woman who wish to live together will simply do so, for as long as they like. Many such informal liaisons flourish even in our own world, and sometimes outlive legitimate marriages. But so long as no children are born, both man and woman are free agents, and the only thing that should hold them together is their love. If children do appear, and are not surrendered for adoption, the couple will be required to sign an agreement accepting mutual responsibility for their upbringing. A measurable fraction of mankind will certainly prefer this modern nuclear family structure to any other, and it will survive as long as they freely choose it, although we must assume that it will quickly lose every trace of the old patriarchal despotism that characterizes all family life in a sexually inequalitarian society.

But most family structures in the new world will be polygamous, in the literal sense of "having many spouses." Group marriage, known to anthropologists in only a few scattered primitive cultures, will thrive in many different forms; indeed, the possibilities are limitless, opening up a world of socializing intimacy and mutual aid far richer than anything within the scope of the nuclear family. Such families may be as small as three persons, or as large as several hundred. Polygyny (many wives) and polyandry (many husbands) will be available to those who prefer arrangements of this sort, as will families composed all of the same sex. But ordinarily the group family will be simply polygamous, composed of several men and several women, who share whatever they agree to share.

What will they share? I can imagine families that will exist primarily to enrich sexual life, or to provide cooperative care of children, or both together. Others may exist primarily for the pursuit of economic and cultural activities: families of farmers, craftsmen, or artists. Some may constitute actual city-states in their own right, whole self-governing communities, politically and economically self-supporting. In some families, sexual monogamy may be the norm, or at least the prevalent form of erotic relationship; others may be sexually polygamous with no permanent pair bonding at all. In either case, it must be repeated that although group families may be formed partly or wholly to facilitate a fuller sexual life for their members, there will be no automatic moral nexus between eroticism, family life, and reproduction in the coming world society. In some families, sexual bonding may not take place at all. By the same token, some families may prefer to share all property communally, and others may not. Some may have children, and others may not.

Will these children of group families be able to grow to adulthood as happily and fulfillingly as in the patriarchal nuclear family? Modern apologists for the old family have invented an elaborate new pseudoreligion that we might call "pedolatry," or child worship. The pedolater believes, or pretends to believe, that the family should be child-centered. Mother and father, but especially mother, must devote long hours every day to the rearing of their children, ready at all times to answer questions, arbitrate disputes, organize play, and conduct educational and recreational family tours for the children's benefit. Children must never be separated from their parents for long periods of time, nor siblings from one another. The mother's education, in particular, is regarded as little more than preparation for her motherly role, so that she can help enlighten her children— even if her education includes one or more university degrees. (I shall not soon forget the many young women at Wellesley College, when I taught history there, who actually believed that they were majoring in history to become better mothers!)

In cold fact, the nuclear family is often as ruinous for children as for spouses. Children are alternately smother-loved and resented by their parents, who begrudge the enormous demands upon their time that young children, by nature self-centered creatures incapable of empathy, will always make, given the opportunity to do so. The child is encouraged to protract his childhood and avoid responsibility for himself as long as possible. He also suffers from the great strains put upon husband and wife by the character of the nuclear marital bond.

The truth of the matter is that there are many more successful ways in which children can be raised, from the system of nursemaids, governesses, tutors, and boarding schools favored by the very wealthy, to the children's homes in Israeli *kibbutzim,* which Bruno Bettelheim finds preferable to the Western system of raising children in separate nuclear families. Children do not need the hourly or daily care of natural parents, although they certainly need care, in varying amounts depending on age, from people who understand them and show them love. The nuclear family with its two or three or four children is a fantastically inefficient device for child rearing; in any case, the majority of mothers and fathers know very little about pedagogy, and have only the most limited natural competence for the task. Cooperative child rearing in group families, or in professionally managed children's homes, will prove much more common than full-time motherhood and fatherhood in the coming social order. The children, far from suffering, will be much happier for it.

Of course nothing is as easy as utopographers make it sound. Many of the new experimental family groups will founder, and none will work perfectly, if only because no system of interpersonal relations can entirely eliminate jealousy and possessiveness and greed. Some may succeed too well, and become no less encapsulated than the nuclear or extended family of tradition, betraying that larger family of mankind to which all men and women owe their final allegiance as social animals. Nonetheless, I am confident that the availability of many different forms of family life will expand human freedom and deepen social consciousness. Perhaps the multiform families of the coming world society will express and undergird its total culture as effectively as the patriarchal nuclear family expresses and undergirds the culture of the dying civilizations of our own age.

CHAPTER SIX

Education

1. Work as Growth

The liberation of womankind, sexual relations, and the family from the iron rule of patriarchism will create styles of interpersonal living quite alien to the traditional cultures and their world views. All the changes we foresee are already visible as moral heresies or countercultural experiments in late twentieth-century America. But these sprouts of new life are still green and tender; they have not yet replaced the patriarchal sexual order, and they will not fully triumph until the coming of the world civilization. The question we must now ask opens up perspectives no less revolutionary. How will men and women work in the new society?

To discuss the place of work in the emerging world culture raises questions that cannot be answered without anticipating, at least briefly, the vision of the world economy offered in the next chapter. But we must anticipate that vision only to show the irrelevancy of the economics of production to the work life of the new culture. Just as the world culture will sever the moral nexus between sex and reproduction, so it will sever the economic nexus between work and production. The ancient need of man to work to feed and clothe and shelter himself will inexorably vanish as the human race evolves toward a "postindustrial" economy. We must assume that automation will continue its progress, to the point foreseen by the Hudson Institute, when only an insignificant fraction of the world's population will be engaged (mostly as technicians) in the production of goods. As Herbert Marcuse argues in *One-Dimensional Man*, the great hope for human freedom is that automation will actually liberate mankind from work, in the sense of labor performed grudgingly for the sheer sake of survival. Automation can also save man from the regimentation that machines impose on their human operators when they are not fully automatic.

But will there be work at all, in such an economy? And what will men and women do with their time, when they are not making love or enjoying their families or raising children? The theorists of postindustrialism assume that the majority of postindustrial workers will be employed in service industries or in specialized arts and crafts, providing with their personal attentions and skills what no automated factory can be programmed to supply. From the economic point of view, these theorists stand obviously on firm ground. The ratio of persons engaged in services rather than production has risen steadily all through modern history, and will continue to rise.

Yet from the cultural point of view, even postindustrialist theory misses the point. It is easy to imagine a vast proliferation of service and crafts industries in which the relationship between man and work would not change, in which economic exploitation of man by man would continue unabated, in which the dehumanizing effects of corporate or governmental giantism would still be felt, and in which man would remain the victim of the logic of his own technique. Breaking the bonds between work and production will require much more than the automation of agriculture and manufacturing. It will require the establishment of a world socialist community of wealth, to be discussed in the next chapter, and it will require the total reconstruction of our view of work.

Although some provision for economic reward of economic labor will continue to be necessary—a system of incentives to encourage whatever work society will need that no free man would otherwise do—the world culture will redefine work to include personal growth and fulfillment. Men and women will work not in the service of material survival, which they can delegate for the most part to a robot machine-culture; nor in the service of the market, which encourages waste and antisocial greed; but in the service of being. They will work to fulfill themselves as servants of being. In so doing, they will help to realize all the highest possibilities latent in their species and in their cosmos. Such is the true work of mankind, which animal necessity kept most of us from undertaking throughout most of recorded history. In the world culture, it will find its proper place at last.

Defined in this sense, work includes even the interpersonal experience described in Chapter Five. Exercising the full range of human erotic powers in loving interaction with other human beings enhances personal growth; the same ends are served by friendship and family relations. When we open our lives to the intimacy of interpersonal union, we bring each other to encounters with being impossible for the isolated self. Also comprehended in work is the self-expression that occurs when we compose or perform works of art or music or literature, or let their creative power vibrate within us, as empathetic viewers or listeners or readers. The participant in any sport who stretches himself to the full, the dancer, the yogi, the explorer, the hermit, are workers.

Finally, work includes education: our function as learners, without which we could not hope to enjoy interpersonal or aesthetic experience, or build any kind of civilization, or conserve and expand our humanity itself. In the coming civilization, no less than half the work of the world, and perhaps much more than half, will consist of education.

2. Learning

Philosophers of education distinguish between education and schooling, and we must begin by drawing the same distinction. In Lessing's phrase, the "education of mankind" involves the whole life of man, the learning by man of his powers and his duties, the growing to maturity of the human race through a great process of searching and discovery. What happens when teachers in schoolrooms instruct students belongs to this process, but it is not all of education. The child learns in the home and the community, as well as in the schoolroom. Most adults continue learning throughout their lives, from their employment, from their families, from the media and the arts and all they do and see. Society learns from its own past experience, and from its success or failure in coping with present problems. Learning takes place in the studies and laboratories of scholars, in museums and libraries, in penitentiaries, on battlefields, anywhere at all, with or without "academic credit."

All this is obvious, even platitudinous. But we must go a step further. In the traditional society, bent on collective defense and survival, most learning has only an instrumental value. Traditional learning prepares populations for "work." But in the postindustrial world society, learning will become an end in itself. A man or woman who does nothing all his life but educate himself, whose sole "product" is his own education, may well have accomplished more than the man or woman whose whole life has been spent in economic labor. It follows that one of the great objectives of a humanized social order must be the making of a race of skilled and knowing human beings: fully realized persons, who understand their condition, and who can contribute to the further enlightenment of the species. To know is to be a man—*Homo sapiens.*

I have suggested that at least half the work of the coming world civilization will consist of education. This means quite simply that the world citizenry will devote at least half of its active hours to learning, both inside and outside, the formal educational structure; and that at least half of those citizens employed in what we call today the "labor force" will be educational workers. Such an estimate may seem utopian when measured against the facts of contemporary life, but I am more likely guilty of excessive caution. First, let us remember that much of the physical and mental labor now performed by human beings will be performed by machines in the coming world society. Also, the ecological crisis will compel a great scaling-down of both production and consumption in the advanced societies, so that many of the jobs now filled by human workers will no longer exist; the work will no longer be done at all. But the decisive consideration is something much more positive: a society that values education can pour limitless human resources into it, without ever reaching a point of diminishing returns. There are literally no limits to the scope of education, or to its capacity for usefully absorbing human energy.

We see this clearly in the history of education in the advanced societies, above all the United States. Two centuries ago, education was restricted to a handful of specially privileged individuals, and even many of these acquired only a few years of formal schooling. Today, nearly the whole American population receives twelve years of formal schooling, and more than half enjoys at least a brief experience of university education. Such statistics would have been dismissed as ludicrous romancing by most eighteenth-century observers, if they had been offered as serious social prophecy by a contemporary. But it is obviously within the means of any industrialized country in the world today to educate all its citizens to the furthest reaches of their natural ability. None has yet chosen to do so, but the prodigious growth of the educational establishment in such countries as the United States and the Soviet Union points the way.

Learning outside such establishments in the coming world civilization will occur in many forms, and will play a far greater part in the lives of its citizens than it does today. Just because extrainstitutional learning is so various and difficult to measure, we can do little more here than predict its continued progress. But the educational establishments themselves will also grow, and not only in the number of students enrolled, or in the number of staff under contract. They will assume new responsibilities, now left to chance or to personal initiative, and they will reach age groups now largely ignored. The schools and universities of the world civilization will become its chief cultural centers, as fundamental to its life as the churches, cathedrals, and monasteries of medieval culture.

Centered on the person rather than on the abstract requirements of the marketplace, the new education will also abandon the military-industrial model of administration now followed in most school systems. Intelligent educators already recognize the inhumanity of modern standardized mass education, with its emphasis on rote learning, its authoritarian styles of administration and instruction, its insensitivity to individual differences, and its tendency to become entangled in self-serving bureaucratic routines. Too often the school administrator or teacher is driven by the exigencies of the system to adopt the mentality of a police chief or a drill sergeant. But as the nexus between work and production dissolves, and as a nearly limitless supply of educational workers becomes available, I foresee a radical qualitative transformation of the whole educational experience.

Teachers, for example, will be able to interact with students on a one-to-one basis. The formal classroom, whether of thirty or three hundred students, will give way to the workshop, the tutorial, the seminar, the open public lecture, and the informal fireside or mealtime dialogue. Many teacher-student meetings will be held outside school buildings: in private homes, in museums, in churches, in offices, in the open air. Individually or in small homogeneous groups, students will advance at their own pace. Standardized curricula and examinations, rigid class schedules, scholarship indexes, and most of the rest of the deadening apparatus of modern education will disappear, as students and teachers arrange their own ways of doing things, to fit their own needs.

By degrees, I also expect that students will become the colleagues, rather than the vassals, of teachers and administrators. They will have a strong, and sometimes deciding, voice on all school and university committees. By the time they are ten or eleven years old, students will act as full partners with their teachers in devising evaluation procedures, teaching strategies, and programs of study. In secondary and higher education, students will have the authority to veto or rescind all faculty and administrative appointments. Those who prefer a more structured or authoritarian system of education may find what they want in certain private schools and universities, but public institutions will stress the development of personal responsibility through the active participation of students in the learning process at all levels. What is unthinkable in modern mass education, oriented toward an all-devouring labor market, will become relatively simple for the schools and universities of a postindustrial world society.

A child's first contact with schooling will probably come during his second or third year, either in the family commune or in schools open to the public. Most very small children learn well and happily in groups of five or ten; they should begin full-time schooling as soon as they can walk and talk. They can learn to read, speak a foreign language, sing, play musical instruments, master simple arithmetic, paint, swim, and much more by the time they are five or six years old, given the right school environment and enough well-trained teachers. The sooner they acquire the basic skills for more advanced learning, the sooner they can begin to think for themselves and cope with the problems and challenges that would most engage their interest in later childhood.

Full-time schooling will continue to at least age twenty-one throughout the world society. The acquisition of skills will remain the main task of the first years of what is now "elementary" education, ages six to ten, but from that point forward the emphasis will shift to education in values, both for self-actualization and for the actualization of the social personality—in Theodore Brameld's phrase, "social-self-realization." The pseudoliberal dogma that young people cannot or should not think about values in the school, and perhaps even outside it, will find few adherents.

All students will be offered essentially the same kind of education through age sixteen, but in the last five years of free universal schooling, I anticipate a separation of students into two main streams of perhaps equal size. The first group will attend undergraduate colleges and receive terminal degrees at age twenty-one. These colleges will play a role in the world society comparable in some ways to that of junior colleges in American higher education or of further education colleges in Great Britain. They will not be "vocational" or "technical" schools, but authentic schools of liberal arts, specially designed to give the benefits of a liberal higher education to all those students who lack the natural gifts to take advantage of university training. Few young people in this group, except some of the less able sons and daughters of the very rich, receive any sort of college education today. For students in need of specialized technical training, institutes will be available at no cost after graduation from college.

The students of the second stream will attend university colleges with a similar, but somewhat more sophisticated program of study until they are twenty-one, and then enter university graduate schools of medicine, law, engineering, administration, fine arts, education, and arts and sciences, very much as they do today. But with the great difference that we are speaking now of at least half the world's population in the third decade of life. Whether a totalizing investment in schooling from earliest childhood, and the eradication of gross inequalities in private wealth and opportunity, can educe such a large number of able minds remains untested. But the American and Soviet experiences strongly suggest that the human ability is there, waiting to be actualized by a caring social order.

The graduates of these professional schools will, for the most part, remain in education all their lives. Some will become teachers, providing a teacher-student ratio at all levels of approximately one to five. Others will enter research; as many as ten percent of the world's population will consist of professional research and development workers, some of whom may also do a certain amount of postgraduate teaching. Still others will become resident artists, writers, musicians, and the like, in numbers so large that no community need ever look far for cultural stimulation. Accomplished creative talents and performers in all media will live no farther away than the nearest university, and there will be universities in almost every community, large or small. Already the United States has more than a thousand reputable universities and university colleges for its two hundred million people. This ratio can be extended to the rest of the world, and improved.

But schooling will not come to an end for anyone, whether at age twenty-one or at age thirty. Citizens from the general population and members of the learning professions will return to educational centers from time to time throughout their lives. A system of sabbatical leaves for advanced study may be introduced, whereby all adult citizens of the world will spend every seventh year in residence at a college or university, pursuing individualized courses of postgraduate study, which may consist of nothing more than intellectual refreshment and the learning of techniques or materials developed since their last time of residence.

None of this involves any necessary change in human nature, or any sudden forward leap in intelligence quotients. At one time, most men were skilled warriors and hunters, and most women cared for infants and made serviceable clothes and pottery. At another time in history, most members of both sexes were peasants, growing rice and wheat and corn. Still later, great numbers of men and women worked in mines and factories. Today, the majority of mankind in the industrialized countries may be found in offices doing "paper work." At each stage in the evolution of work, different skills were required; different personality types were encouraged. I see no reason to doubt the possibility that in the coming world civilization, the largest number of men and women will be teachers and scholars.

Nor should we worry about the strain that such an increase in educational facilities might place upon the world economy. Education costs relatively little. For the most part it consists of encounters between human beings, or between human beings and such artifacts of culture as books or laboratory apparatus. The artifacts may sometimes prove expensive, but the human beings will offer their services for whatever the world economy can afford to give them, as they have always done. Since the world of the future will be as rich in human resources as it will be poor in natural resources, I can think of no more practical, as well as humanizing, focus of work life for our dawning planetary order.

3. Schools and Values

We must now retrace our steps, and look more closely at the work of the schools and undergraduate colleges, which will provide formal learning opportunities for young people from their second to twenty-first years.

Certainly the great task of the schools in the first ten years of life must be to bring the child up from simple animal existence to the threshold of full humanity, by teaching him the skills he will need for all further learning and by socializing his consciousness deeply enough that he will be ready to live in a world of many billions of interdependent human beings. No school system today performs these tasks adequately, least of all the American, which tends to treat all young children as if they were mentally retarded. The average small child can be taught to read before he is six; he can master several foreign languages if he has teachers or parents who speak to him regularly in these languages; he can accumulate and use a vocabulary several times larger than anything attempted in traditional graded readers; before he is ten, he can assimilate all the principles of arithmetic and simple algebra and geometry. Fast-paced multimedia instruction with the aid of teaching machines and a reward system for the reinforcement of individual achievement can vastly accelerate the learning of basic skills.

At the same time, small children need to have their minds stretched by the gradual introduction into their educational experience of the basic concepts of the sciences and the humanities. Some children are ready sooner than others for high-order conceptual thinking, and separation into achievement groups will be necessary both in skill training and concept formation, to capitalize on the strengths of individual children and also to detect and overcome individual weaknesses at the earliest possible level.

But most children can learn to cope with large concepts at a surprisingly young age. They are especially quick to grasp some of the elementary concepts and insights of astronomy, physics, biology, geography, and anthropology. A world-minded educational system will lose no time giving its young children the broadest possible conceptual framework. It will come to stars, planets, the elements, the states of matter, evolution, the nature of life, the taxonomy of life forms, the races and sexes of mankind, and world cultures and geography long before it reaches the minutiae of national history, regional rivers, or the anatomy of the local firehouse.

In the second decade, ages eleven to twenty-one, young people will grow much further, from the brave beginnings made in elementary school. They will perfect their skills, more fully develop their conceptual powers, and clothe the concepts they have mastered with the flesh of relevant cognitive data. But even then the learning of skills and concepts will take precedence over the learning of information. As Jerome Bruner and other educational psychologists have shown, the key to the understanding of any scientific discipline is a grasp of its fundamental concepts and principles of organization. It is only in this second decade, also, that young people will develop enough sense of time and change to learn something of the course of world history, a discipline that Bruner misunderstands, and to which his recommendations do not fully apply. We shall have more to say about the special place of history in the educational process at the end of this chapter.

But the most decisive aspect of secondary and undergraduate education, as I have already indicated, will be the study of values. In traditional pedagogy, values are either imposed with a heavy hand or ignored with a fine show of scholarly detachment and liberal tolerance. Neither attitude catches the spirit of the world culture, or its pedagogy. The schools will manage, as they must, to fuse the authoritarian and liberal views in a higher synthesis that respects both the holy worldliness of universal civilization and the moral autonomy of the valuing self.

Values come in a variety of forms: instrumental and absolute; moral and religious; intellectual and aesthetic. The common denominator of all these forms of value is the determination of that which ought to be, as opposed to that which is. Values define what is good and beautiful, what is right and just, how men should think and feel, how they should live, alone and together. Our struggle in these chapters to picture the ideal world civilization is an exercise in valuing. If the essence of a culture lies in its system of values, an educational system indifferent to the problem of value is a system dead in the heart and dead in the mind.

The schools of the coming world civilization will enter upon the study of values with three goals in mind: to inform, to clarify, and to acculturate. The first two are familiar to any liberal reader as goals of progressivist education today. The objective description of past and present value systems opens up to the student at any age level a range of possibilities from which he may choose, while at the same time it helps to complete his knowledge of history and modern civilization. If the study of values goes no further than such description, it remains just as empirical as the study of planetary orbits or insect life cycles. But the second realm of axiological inquiry, value clarification, will challenge students to become moralists themselves, to define their own value commitments. Nothing is more essential to the development of personhood than the creation of a personal axiological identity, a task that is hampered or blocked more often than it is encouraged by traditional pedagogy.

Yet the world culture can no better afford than any historic culture to remain silent about its own values. However much latitude of belief and conduct it allows its individuals, it must seek to enclose them within its own cultural parameters. It must seek to enlist them in its own historically evolved patterns of common life and service. The schools in this second decade will have a unique responsibility to evangelize on behalf of the world civilization—on behalf of its religion, ethical culture, system of interpersonal relations, laws, government, and economy. Such evangelism can be called indoctrination; certainly the world civilization will have its propaganda, its message that must be passed on to the next generation. If it believes in itself, it will not keep this faith a secret for its high priests alone.

But acculturation can avoid authoritarianism, both within and outside the educational structure. The world society will not allow itself the dangerous power of imposing its beliefs on any man by force, by threats, or by discrimination. World constitutional law will protect every citizen against the rape of his conscience by public authority. In the schools, the values of the world culture will be presented sympathetically by at least some teachers in each institution, although other teachers may hold opposed views. Free discussion will define the degree of dissent from world values for each student, if such dissent exists, and alternative values from minority cultures or past societies will be openly debated. Since world patriotism will be a liberal doctrine in its own right, open to change, tolerant of peaceful dissent, and productive of much individual diversity even within its own frontiers, I think it will succeed in quietly disarming most of its opposition without much struggle, but sometimes it will have to enter the fray quite fervently. At all odds, it must be skilled in the arts of ideological warfare, and it must evince a strong will to survive. No culture can long endure without a transcendent sense of its own world mission.

The values of the world culture will also be transmitted to students indirectly through the integrative strategies adopted for the teaching of all subjects, whether axiological or not. In traditional education, the student learns bodies of information, disciplines, and skills in relatively isolated segments, often for no other reason than because they are considered good intellectual exercise. I would expect educators in the world society to devote a substantial portion of the curriculum, especially in the last ten years of schooling, to programs that bring many disciplines into vigorous interaction in order to explain man, his society, and his cosmos as holistic systems. Indeed, one of the great tasks for research in the world's universities will be to achieve a working synthesis of all the disciplines; most efforts to teach interdisciplinary courses in schools and colleges today fail because no such synthesis actually exists.

In place of separate courses in history, social science, literature, psychology, philosophy, and the arts, picture a program of study that might be known simply as "Civilization," in which the concepts, insights, and methods of each discipline are fused. Students learn to perceive the world civilization as a single interlocking structure of thought and action. Upon the images of political man, economic man, national man, and the rest, is superimposed an image of the whole man, whose life is touched by all the activities of civilization. Topics chosen for specialized treatment reveal the interplay of these activities in specific life situations, such as the planning of a city, the drafting of a constitution, or the building of a university. As individuals or in teams, students confront problems drawn from the world in which they actually live, problems for which they must work out experimental solutions based on their own systems of value. Educators may also devise similar integrative programs to bring together the learning of the natural sciences, and to harmonize the natural sciences at a still higher level of integration with the learning of the sciences of man.

But from the axiological point of view, the chief significance of such programs would be their resonance with the values of the world culture itself. The thrust of integrative studies is always upward, toward world and cosmos. Even when values are not introduced into such studies, or when students are not asked to formulate and apply their own values, they acquire a perspective that is dynamically holistic, a perspective from which it becomes difficult to resist the overarching values of the world culture discussed in Chapter Four. When a student learns to see life from national standpoints alone, even if no direct attempt is made to convert him to nationalism, he tends to develop a value system congruent with national interests. His mind is closed to the world, of which he knows little or nothing. An education that stresses the planetary and cosmic scope of life and being will tend to produce minds that can embrace the whole universe. What we know is not necessarily what we love and protect; but what we do not know, we cannot love at all.

The aim of all learning in the world culture, both in the cognitive and affective domains, will be the actualization of the person, as an individual with an existence of his own (Martin Heidegger's *Dasein*) and as a social being. Yet, all such actualization depends ultimately and most deeply on the development of an axiological identity, a personality capable of free, conscious, and intelligent value decisions. No culture can set a higher goal for its schools.

4. The Free Academy

Few institutions in modern society have acquired as many functions and meanings as the university. From one perspective, the modern university is primarily a vocational training school, designed to supply industry, government, and the professions with high-level technicians. In many American communities the university serves primarily as a gladiator show; the only buildings on campus not expendable are the football stadium and the basketball arena. The university is also a great marriage market for middle-class and aristocratic youth, a community service center, and—in radical eyes—a recruitment facility for the Revolution.

Academicians are often tempted to wag their heads and think back to centuries gone by when universities adhered to their "proper" business. Dwight Waldo speaks of the myth of the "True University," a familiar theme at any faculty meeting devoted to large issues. "Sometimes," he notes, "faculty members engage in flights of pious rhetoric about the True University as though it were a Platonic form or a medieval essence. Sometimes the True University is conceived to have existed in fact in times past —when professors were giants in the earth." But for Waldo, who prefers not to play games with history, the university has always been "established and supported by, and as an adjunct to, the established order." It has always been utilitarian, never a free and pure community of philosophic scholars.

Waldo's point is well taken. The first Western universities, in the Middle Ages, were schools of law, medicine, or theology reinforced by faculties of arts and sciences. Throughout history, the university has served the immediate interests and needs of the society in which it flourished. The much reviled American practice of supplementing traditional academic and professional programs with colleges of education, business administration, engineering, and the like, harmonizes in every way with the historic role of the university.

In the world civilization, universities—no less than schools—will minister to the social order. They cannot do otherwise. They will train specialists in all those fields that require long and relatively arduous professional education. They will assist and interact with government and industry. But for the first time in the history of the university, its primary function will be to provide a sanctum for research as an end in itself. What has been at most a genteel Hellenic myth will become an earnest reality, not because the university will cease to serve society, but because society will at last value productive scholarship as one of its reasons for being. The discovery of knowledge for the pure joy of knowing will take its place as a great practical need of civilized mankind, employing more men and women than either industry or government.

But before we look more closely at the work of the universities, let us try to imagine the scale and proportions of the university system in the world society. As we noted above, the student population is likely to divide into two streams after age sixteen, the first attending terminal undergraduate colleges, the second receiving five years of advanced liberal education at university colleges. The university college will offer essentially the same education in values and general knowledge provided by other colleges, but in addition it will administer special preprofessional trial programs to familiarize students with the work of its various graduate schools.

It is here, in the graduate schools, that the life of the university will center. They will be much larger than the graduate institutions of today, not only because all holders of degrees in the university colleges will normally enter them (as well as late-blooming students transferring by special examination from the colleges of the first "stream"), but also because their faculties will include great numbers of resident research scholars and artists. Hundreds of thousands of universities will exist throughout the world, with perhaps a quarter of the world's population directly associated in their communal life, as students, teaching and research fellows, artists, librarians, and administrative staff. At the same time, the need for individual universities to become impersonal giants on the model of the universities of Paris, New York, or Tokyo will disappear as universities agree on a world basis to avoid needless duplication of effort in research requiring costly facilities, and as complete microform libraries of all the world's pictorial and written materials become available everywhere at a small fraction of the expense of original documents. I envisage a vast process of academic decentralization that will enrich the life of every community, and make good universities as ubiquitous as shopping centers or factories today.

Not that each university will be a carbon copy of every other. In addition to public universities sponsored by the world commonwealth, other universities will flourish under the auspices of churches, educational cooperatives, and private foundations. Each will have its special research interests, its own pedagogical style, and its own system of self-governance. Some will shelter a complete range of professional schools, others may limit themselves to a few, or offer work only in the arts and sciences. Some will accept government commissions to institute studies in public policy and research in technical and economic problems of urgent public interest; others will remain aloof from the immediate affairs of the world commonwealth.

But one vital concern all the universities of the world society will share: a concern for their freedom of inquiry, whether in the classroom, the laboratory, or in publications. This is one ancient ideal of the academy that must carry over into the universities of the world civilization. At the furthest frontiers of research and thought in all fields, a point must be defined where the world culture itself is left behind, and the scholar enters the void of ignorance with a mind as wide open as he can pry it, as bare of values as he can strip it, to discover what he can by reason, experience, and intuition alone.

Here we return to our beginning theme: the primary function of the university as a sanctum for pure research—let us dare to call it *wertfrei*, or "value-free," research. In modern societies, value-free academicism is too often a way of escaping social responsibility or concealing a tacit commitment to the established order. But in the world city of our vision, the professional standards of scientific scholarship first clearly set in the universities of the nineteenth century will become nothing more or less than they should be: canons of dispassionate truthfulness, pledges by the scholar that he will do all in his power to make an honest search for knowledge.

It goes without saying that no scholar is bound by his pledge of value neutrality to abandon his own personal values when he is not acting in a professional capacity. But an immense gap separates the entrenched ideologue who finds only what he wants to find, and the honest scholar who lets the chips fall where they may, even if sometimes his preconceptions or loyalties influence their fall against his conscious will. The ideologue-scholar is a fraud, who betrays his calling and gives his fellow man less than full measure. He learns nothing that he has not been programmed to learn. Except by the rarest coincidences, only the value-free scholar can discover new truth and find personal fulfillment in his vocation.

This is a hard position to take in a time of imminent world disaster. Universities today have quite properly begun to turn their attention to the question of how mankind shall be saved. Many students and younger instructors have lost faith in the ideal of professionalism, and sometimes even in the doctrine of academic freedom. But a peaceful and unified world will find the tradition of value-free scholarship worth reviving, and perfecting. The importance of such scholarship to the personal integrity of the scholar and to science can hardly be doubted; but it is also entirely credible that the world culture itself will die if it is not refreshed from time to time by the sap of new knowledge and new intellectual perspectives. Just as we must ensure freedom of thought and belief to all men and women in the world order, so we must ensure the absolute freedom of the scholar to pursue his research as his calling leads him, uncensored by public authority in any form.

The tension between personal value commitment and scholarly detachment, as between theocracy and liberty, will be difficult to maintain without the collapse of one or the other. No thriving culture has ever been able to resist the temptation to impose its values by a mixture of force and suasion on unbelievers, including scholars who arrive at inconvenient discoveries. One thinks, for example, of Wilhelmian Germany, the home of the greatest universities of the nineteenth century, the Germany of Ranke and Weber; yet, in no country did the academic intelligentsia prostitute itself so enthusiastically to the service of the imperial state in its classrooms. The same professors by and large capitulated to the pedagogical demands of the Nazis in the 1930's. Scholarship has been in chains in Soviet Russia since at least the Stalin era. It fares no better in Maoist China. The somewhat greater freedom in the West, which is often more illusory than real, may owe as much to the rapid deterioration of traditional value systems in the West as to the positive influence of liberal thought. But everywhere the scholar is given to understand that he is paid to do his job in a manner pleasing to his society. Let the honest man beware!

To Dwight Waldo's charge that there has never been a free academy, let us therefore reply: yes, but it will one day exist. The universities of the world order, and above all their graduate schools, will at last become true communities of scholars, guilds of masters and apprentices dedicated to the honorable arts of scholarship, content if their work be well done, no matter what its "commercial" value in the outside world. Such esoteric goals must seem naive today, but in a society where most of the labor necessary to human survival and comfort is performed by self-regulating machines, and all men and women are educated to the limits of their educability, they will become fully serious for the first time.

5. Cognitive Synthesis

We have still to discuss one task of value-free scholarship that may engage the attention of a relatively small number of minds, and yet bears the highest significance for the progress of research, for effective teaching, and even for the building of the world culture. Philosophers define this task as "cognitive synthesis." Or we may call it the integration of human knowledge, the orchestration of the various knowledge-gathering disciplines into a unified system with interacting and mutually comprehensible methodologies and languages.

Several twentieth-century scholars, including Lancelot Law Whyte, Otto Neurath, and Oliver L. Reiser, have attempted to achieve cognitive synthesis by working upward from the physical sciences. A great French synthesist, Henri Berr, sought the new queen of the sciences in historiography. Dialectical materialism supplies a ground for synthesis in Marxist thought. The search for synthesis in Western intellectual history goes back, through Spencer and Comte, to Hegel, Comenius, and Bacon, and still further, to Aquinas and finally Aristotle. But the need for synthesis has never been so acute as in the twentieth century. Never before has Western man's demonic analytical genius resulted in such intensive specialization of scholarly labor, and given rise, as José Ortega y Gasset pointed out, to so many educated barbarians with such fragmented world views.

The disunity of knowledge and the anarchic relationship among the sciences in the twentieth century can be held at least partly responsible for the spiritual crisis in modern Western culture, and in all cultures strongly affected by Western scholarship. When the analytical approach is applied "exclusively and unrestrictedly," writes Erich Kahler, when it lacks "the control of organized synthesis, then it is bound to lead into disintegration of our knowledge, our mind, and our very life." And "a unified picture of our world . . . is the indispensable prerequisite to the formation of a human community."

Kahler may exaggerate the importance of cognitive synthesis to the growth of cultures, but clearly a world culture rooted in holistic concepts of personhood, mankind, and cosmos would receive much needed support for its life creed in a scheme for the integration of human knowledge that satisfied both logic and experience. No rational bridge connects fact and value, and yet a culture that strives for wholeness in values will also strive for wholeness in knowledge, because wholeness itself is one of its highest values.

But this is to speak as a moralist, rather than as a scholar. Although the search for cognitive synthesis may to some degree be initiated by moral or spiritual considerations, as Aquinas was moved by a pious wish to harmonize Aristotle with Christian doctrine, value-free scholarship can justify such a search in only one way. Synthesis is academically worth seeking because it will further the cause of scholarship, either by making readily accessible to workers in each field the results of relevant research elsewhere, or by facilitating authentically interdisciplinary studies. Most disciplines have something to offer most other disciplines, but efforts to fuse their learning typically fail, for lack of a Rosetta stone that can translate the methods, concepts, and language of one discipline into those of any other. Correlations go unseen. Work is needlessly duplicated. Because each university department is a sovereign state, answerable only to itself, programs are designed with no sense of their relationship to one another; instructors have no colleagues, and students no advisers, to answer their questions if they should ever wonder what relationships actually exist.

How far the integration of knowledge can be carried remains to be tested. The value-free researcher cannot predict what he will discover. Perhaps he will learn that his task is wrongly conceived and must be formulated in terms quite unlike those suggested here. Or integration may be impossible to achieve, in the very nature of things. More plausibly, the researcher may develop several alternative schemes for synthesis, growing out of alternative initial premises or logics. The competition of rival programs for cognitive synthesis may conceivably become the chief form of academic warfare in the new culture, replacing the feuds within and between disciplines in our own. But only when universities throughout the world at last invest their energies in a serious effort to end the intellectual anarchy that they have done so much themselves to create, will we know to what extent our hopes for the establishment of an ordered academic cosmos can be fulfilled.

Certainly cognitive synthesis will require an enormous commitment of time and thought on the part of thinkers in every field. It will also very likely require the emergence of a new kind of specialist: the specialist in integration, who may be a philosopher, or who may evade disciplinary affiliations altogether. The professional synthesist is a scholar who does not even properly exist in twentieth-century academe. But the world universities of the future may well establish institutes, departments, even colleges of cognitive synthesis, to engage in basic research and to bring scholars of all fields into active rapport. A similar suggestion was made many years ago by Ortega y Gasset in his *Mission of the University*, the idea of a permanent "Faculty of Culture," which would serve as the "nucleus" of the university and of higher learning generally. Ortega foresaw the staffing of such faculties by "a kind of scientific genius which hitherto has existed only as an aberration: the genius for integration."

In the end, this new race of specialists may be forced to lead an "ecumenical movement" in academic life that will reduce drastically the num-

---

ber of disciplines. Only disciplines whose distinctive outlook and methodology prove their worth after searching evaluation by professional synthesists will be able to survive as autonomous fields of study. Nor will the survivors coexist "democratically" in the unstructured anarchy that prevails today. One of the foremost tasks of our synthesists will be to show how the disciplines interlock, not as points on a line, or as lines in a plane figure, but as fields of concentration in a multidimensional thought world, entering that world from different angles, moving in different directions, and influencing one another in many different ways. Some are actually satellites of larger fields. Others pursue a more independent course.

Such images would not be necessary if we were thinking only of a positivist hierarchy of the sciences in the manner of Auguste Comte or the "Unity of Science" movement that originated in the 1930's in Viennese logical positivism. The so-called positive sciences, from physics and biology to psychology and sociology, order sensory knowledge through the construction of heuristic devices of more or less general applicability, such as laws, models, and ideal types. To bring all of these disciplines into full communication with one another, and even to reconcile conflicting theories and schools of thought within given disciplines, such as Freudian and Pavlovian psychology or quantum and field physics, will take much patient work. But the synthesis I envisage must also incorporate disciplines outside the modern Western positivist tradition. Not all knowledge is from the senses. The scientist's universally valid theory is not the only way to organize knowledge.

How, for example, will our synthesists cope with the kind of knowledge or truth provided by the humanistic student of art and literature; by the Christian theologian and the Buddhist metaphysician; by the existentialist philosopher and the Sufi poet; or by the historian?

History offers the especially difficult case of a discipline that is both an empirical science and an ancient representative of the humanities. It resembles the social sciences in its dependence on first-hand sensory experience, which it seeks to interpret objectively. But it is also an antinomian science: except for sociologizing historians like Toynbee, its practitioners are typically concerned with the reconstruction and explanation of events as they actually happen, in all their existential uniqueness and concreteness. They have no interest in discovering laws of universal applicability. They do not attempt to formulate abstract definitions of man or society.

Their ultimate purpose is closer to that of the realistic novelist or tone poet: to capture in a linear flow of thought the peculiar truth of specific happenings in human time.

Yet history, in its own way, is no less universalistic than philosophy or science, for historians insist upon seeing the interdependence of events in their historical contexts, and the ultimate unity of all contexts in the web of world history. They perceive this unity concretely in terms of events unfolding in real time, not as abstractions in the theoretical component of knowledge. To bring historicism and positivism into the same "ordered academic cosmos" without destroying the essential qualities of either will be far more difficult than many scholars who preach the interdisciplinary approach seem to realize.

All the same, we may reasonably hope that this and many other problems just as terrifying are ultimately soluble. If cognitive synthesis can be achieved, in one way or in several, all disciplines will communicate and interact freely across any professional frontiers that survive. We must look forward to the day when the knowledge of the mystic will be integrated with the knowledge of the psychologist, when sociology and chemistry will flourish in the same universe of discourse, when economists will be able to communicate with art historians, and behaviorists with neo-Aristotelians. The unity of world culture will be strengthened, teaching at all levels will acquire deeper relevance to life, and research will thrive as never before.

CHAPTER SEVEN

Commonwealth

1. Power and Plenitude

The conventional utopia is a vision of the ideal government and economy, a vision of power justly wielded and wealth widely shared. There may also be glimpses of the arts and sciences, of education, of home and family life; but the essence of the utopia is its view of how man survives in his perennial struggle with nature and his fellow man. The peace movement, international socialism, and world federalism focus most of their attention on the same problem. Yet in this book we devote only one chapter to government and economics, and we place it near the end, as if such things had no more than marginal significance in a world civilization.

But perhaps this is all they should have. Although the struggle for power and wealth has dominated the history of mankind so far, world integration means world pacification: the replacement of struggle, so far as possible, by worldwide social discipline and technological control of the material conditions of life. Power is no more than a means to the service of being. Once mankind has passed safely through the era of competing nation-states and machines have taken the place of men as workers, politics and economics will lose much of their human relevance. At least half the energy now given to politics and economics will be reinvested in what we have defined broadly as culture: in art and science, drama and literature, sport and travel, scholarship and craftsmanship, religion and interpersonal relations.

This does not mean the end of human greed, or competitiveness, or aggression; it does not mean the transmutation of men into angels or sheep. All it signifies is the close of that long era in human history when the contest for governmental power and material wealth were in some degree necessary to our progress, and even to our survival as a species. In the twentieth century, these primordial struggles have become counterproductive. If allowed to continue, they will lead inevitably to the destruction of the species. The only rational alternative is a socialist world commonwealth, ensuring peace, equality, democracy, and the freedom of all men and women to seek fulfillment in harmony with cosmic being. The world commonwealth will supply the indispensable material preconditions for the secure growth of the world culture. Yet, once established, this governmental and economic system by its very nature will absorb less human energy than any comparable system in history. For the most part, it will be self-regulating. Just as most of the heat has already been removed from domestic and foreign politics in such relatively pacified parts of the world as Scandinavia, Switzerland, and New Zealand, and just as the peoples of many preindustrial societies enjoy relative immunity from the obsessive acquisitiveness of the modern era, so the inhabitants of the postindustrial City of Man will need no civil or world wars and no upward spiraling economic "growth" rate to give them a sense of purpose in life. They will look for fulfillment (and fortune) elsewhere.

At the same time, we must not imagine a society without government or economic activity. The world commonwealth will not be any the less real because it lacks the glamour of its counterparts in the civilizations of the twentieth century. The need for government and for an economic system that supplies all mankind with the means of subsistence will remain. Anyone who dreams of benevolent anarchy and self-sustaining small agriculture as a way of life for a planet that will house twelve billion human beings (the probable world population by the middle of the next century) is more than a romantic: he is a purveyor of fraudulent and worthless hopes. We shall need a government. We shall need it to ensure the democratic distribution of wealth, to prevent crime and rehabilitate criminals, to educate the world citizenry, to curtail population growth, to plan and administer the world industrial complex, to manage the natural environment responsibly, to guard against counterrevolution and civil warfare, and to sponsor mankind's exploration of the universe. We shall also need an economic order that can make the best of the earth's dwindling resources and keep us alive and well until new technologies emerge that may once more permit a rising standard of material life—if such a thing ever becomes possible again, and if we still want it when it does.

I look forward, then, to a commonwealth charged with great responsibilities, although it will need a much smaller investment of human energy than states and economies have ever demanded before in world history. It will touch all of life, and upon its smooth functioning will depend everything that the world civilization can hope to accomplish.

Fortified by the unfolding world will of the universal culture, our commonwealth will at last be able to put into effect those technological solutions to the problems of mankind that we rejected in Chapter Two. In the 1970's, such solutions are like power tools without a power source. But in a postrevolutionary world commonwealth, they become eminently practicable. I share the strongest enthusiasm of the most innocent scientific utopist when it is a question of applying technological solutions in a liberated world civilization; in such a context, the fetters upon imagination fall away, and we lose all sense of limits.

The feasibility of world government itself, regardless of context, is often questioned by conservative sceptics. They argue not only that vested political interests will prevent its coming, which is certainly a reasonable contention, but also that a government with a jurisdiction so vast would be impossible to construct, which is clearly absurd. Given at least the vigorous beginnings of a world culture, a world state is no more difficult to envisage than the states of our own time. These modern states are guilty of all sorts of inhumanity, yet in other respects they serve the commonweal more ably than any premodern civilized polity could have hoped to do. They are more efficient, not less, than the states of antiquity. They distribute wealth more equitably. They maintain civil peace more dependably. They permit as much, and sometimes more, personal freedom. Although their lines of communication are often thousands of miles long, and some of them claim hundreds of millions of citizens, they have already solved nearly all the technical problems that hobbled the effectiveness of large polities in the past. What can be done on the scale of a continent, can be done (and with deeper humanity, done better) on the scale of a planet.

In the same way, there are no insuperable barriers to the creation of an integrated world economy in which all regions are equally well developed, and the means of a decent life are available to all men and women. The relative luxury enjoyed by millions in the technologically advanced countries of the twentieth century will be impossible to maintain in those countries or extend to other parts of the planet for an indefinite period of time. But if our world will is strong enough, and the sovereign people delegate all necessary authority to their world government, we have enough ingenuity to prevent ecological disaster and provide for the basic needs of mankind.

It is all a question of priorities. If we decide to manage, rather than squander, the natural resources left to us; if we submit to rational population planning; if we can agree to a program for balanced world economic development, we have nothing to fear. In due course technology will find new sources of energy and raw materials to replace or even improve upon those now being exploited. The total automation of industry and agriculture will liberate man from depersonalizing labor in all its forms.

Such drastic changes are clearly beyond reach without an authentic world revolution. We cannot destroy the regime of established power without the use of countervailing power. Yet the commonwealth we must build in place of all contemporary polities will be the expression of a culture that no longer places a high valuation on economic and political power. The day of the bespangled warrior, the Machiavellian potentate, and the corporate pirate draws to a close. In Dane Rudhyar's phrase, we seek an age not of plenty, but of plenitude, a more tranquil time in the history of the species, when every man's goal is enjoyment of the fullness of being, and every man helps to fulfill being in the inmost fastness of his life.

2. The World State

The world state, as I foresee it, will be unitary, democratic, socialist, and liberal. Unitary, because sovereign power is indivisible; democratic, because the general will is sovereign, and oligarchies, technocracies, and dictatorships are more vulnerable to corruption than an enlightened mass electorate; socialist, because private capital is monopolistic by nature and tends to usurp the authority and wealth of the people; and liberal, because the end of all government is to set men free to become what they choose to become in conformity with the unique conditions of their own being.

Since any of these ideas, pushed to its logical conclusions, might accomplish the destruction of the other three, the constitution of the world state must be finely balanced, a masterpiece of political and legal art beyond one mind's power to conceive. The suggestions that follow are intended

only to provoke thought, and should not be interpreted as a literal prophecy of things to come. For the sake of argument, I also assume that most of
mankind will survive the great crises still separating us from the arrival of
the world civilization, and that we are speaking of a point in time approximately one century from now, after the revolution that ends the nation-
state system, but before the world civilization has reached maturity or un-
done all the inequities of the old order. In the event of a major world catastrophe that obliterates most of the species, any world commonwealth that
emerged from the wreckage would at first necessarily take a quite different
form, although it might one day grow to resemble our model fairly closely.

Unlike most proposed world polities, ours is not a federation of the existing sovereign nation-states. It is not a federation at all, but a unitary republic of mankind, and we cannot go further in describing it until this point is
made absolutely clear. A union of historic nation-states, large, small, rich,
poor, each vying to safeguard its political identity and its "sovereignty,"
could be no more than the last chapter in the story of the old civilizations.
I cannot imagine a union of this sort coming into existence at all. To make
a federation out of such mismatched entities as the United States, the Mal-
dive Islands, Pakistan, Norway, China, and Nicaragua would call for political sorcery of the highest order.

But the gravest objection to federalism is that it perpetuates the nation-
state system in a new form. Even if all parts of the world were equally
prosperous, and all nations were the same size, or the smallest powers
amalgamated with their neighbors to form appreciably bigger states, federation would still have the effect of preserving obsolescent state forms and
consecrating the status quo. Traditional quarrels could be renewed at any
time, and civil wars on the model of 1861–65 in America would replace
world wars on the model of 1914–18 or 1939–45.

If we have an authentically new civilization, it will be far better to dissolve most of the political frontiers of the old civilizations, and begin
afresh. For purposes of local self-government and world elections, the
planet may be partitioned into constituencies of approximately five million
people each, the size of Chicago or Scotland or the Azerbaidzhan Republic. Some will be cities, others large rural districts, still others combinations
of the two. The obvious precedent is the division of France into departments by the National Assembly during the Revolution. To the democratically elected governments of the constituent districts, the world constitu-

tion will delegate limited powers of home rule, but all powers not specifically entrusted to the districts will be reserved to the world commonwealth and to the people.

The government of the commonwealth will consist of four branches: a unicameral legislature (the World Assembly), an executive council selected by the World Assembly (the World Council), a judiciary (the World Court, together with world benches of original jurisdiction in each district, and courts of appeals for every three districts), and a tribunate (the World Chamber of Tribunes), charged with supervisory responsibilities and the provision of legal and ombudsman services for private individuals, consumers' groups, the institutions of minority cultures, and others in need of special protection from abuses of public power. The world constitution must ensure that each of these branches is in some measure independent of the others, so that no single branch can draw to itself the full authority of the commonwealth.

The great size of the commonwealth will make direct election of the World Assembly by the people impractical, but this obstacle can be overcome by the establishment of an electoral college system, which will assume responsibility for choosing both the World Assemblymen and the World Tribunes. Each constituent district will elect five electors by universal suffrage, who will join forces with the electors of two other districts (comprising an electoral region) to select one Assemblyman and one Tribune. If we assume an initial world population of twelve billion people, and constituent districts of five million each, this gives us a World Assembly of eight hundred members, and a World Chamber of the same size.

The Assembly and the Chamber will enjoy a dialectical relationship to one another. The Assembly is the legislative body; it will also choose the World Council, whose members will be responsible at all times to the Assembly; and since the Council in turn will appoint the highest-ranking judges and the heads of all government ministries, the Assembly will have direct or indirect control over every branch of government except the Chamber. I see the World Chamber of Tribunes under these circumstances as much more than an independent agency to investigate private complaints against the exercise of public power, although this will surely be one of its most important functions. It will act almost as an alternative government, somewhat like the Petrograd Soviet in the summer of 1917 in Russia. The Chamber will have the power and responsibility to arrange for independent audits of public accounts; it will maintain close surveillance

over all the activities of the other three branches; it will bring suits against
government officials; it will introduce legislation into the World Assembly
in special cases, and such legislation will become law unless at least three-
fifths of the Assemblymen vote to reject it. Tribunes, however, will also be
subject to impeachment by the World Assembly and trial by the World
Court.

The World Council, a body of twenty-five chosen for five-year terms by
the Assembly, but not from its own membership, will act as the collective
head of state; the presidency of the Council will rotate once every ten
weeks, and every Councilman will be the peer of every other. The Council
will exercise general supervision over the ministries of state, and make final
policy decisions in all but routine matters. I foresee at least seven great
ministries, most of whose day-to-day work will be performed by computer
complexes requiring little human supervision.

We shall need a ministry of finance to keep the accounts of the world
commonwealth and collect its revenues. The ministry of justice will en-
force the laws of the commonwealth and restore offenders to society
through its rehabilitation programs. The ministry of education will oversee
the vast system of public instruction, and award accreditation to private
schools; it will also be responsible for the promotion of the creative and
performing arts, since most artists will have residencies at the world's colleges and universities. In the same way, the ministry of education will
serve as the principal patron of scholarly and scientific research.

Two departments will share responsibility for the economic life of the
commonwealth: the ministries of welfare and ecology. Welfare will manage the world's automated factories, mines, farms, construction facilities,
food and department stores; it will supply every citizen with a guaranteed
annual basic income, and it will maintain a complete system of public
health care. But we shall also require a ministry of ecology to work with
the ministry of welfare in preventing environmental spoliation, developing
alternative sources of raw materials, and administering the world population policy.

Finally, we shall have a ministry of space, to conduct the programs of
the commonwealth for the exploration and colonization of outer space;
and a ministry of security, to maintain public peace. A world security force
of at least one hundred thousand professional troops, drawn from all regions of the commonwealth and equipped to fly at short notice to any part
of the planet, will probably be needed for many years, to cope with local

violence or the possibility of armed insurrection at the district or world level. No other armies, and no other armed formations of any kind except small district and community police forces, will lawfully exist in the world commonwealth. None other will be needed.

In addition to appointing the heads of these seven departments of state, the World Council will also select the justices of the World Court, who will sit for life terms. Modern experience suggests the great value of an independent judiciary, and it will be all the more desirable in a state that otherwise concentrates so much power in its legislature. The judges of the regional courts of appeals will be appointed for terms of fifteen years by the ministry of justice, and the judges of the district courts of original jurisdiction for terms of ten years by the district governments, subject to the approval of the ministry of justice.

The World Court, as in the "Preliminary Draft of a World Constitution" published by the Hutchins Committee at the University of Chicago in 1948, will consist of several benches. The Chicago Draft specified five benches of twelve justices each, the first to deal with constitutional issues arising from disputes between organs of the world government itself, the second to resolve conflicts between the world government and local jurisdictions, the third to hear cases involving the world government and private citizens. Where world law applied, the fourth bench considered disputes between local jurisdictions and citizens, the fifth considered disputes between citizens. This division of judicial labor, or one very similar to it, will be adopted for the World Court of our future commonwealth.

But of course a plan of government, taken by itself, means very little. If the constitution proposed here became the law of the planet, it might lead to tyranny worse than anything now known by mankind; or it might lead to chaos and the eventual disintegration of the world commonwealth. The world government so established could be ultrabureaucratic, or excessively vulnerable to political pressure. Although it would be naive to suppose that free men can live together peaceably without governmental institutions of some kind, more important than the institutions of the commonwealth are its laws and the relations of production that it fosters and legitimizes. To these, we turn next.

3. The Law of Citizenship

Since medieval times Western man has devised many written contracts detailing the privileges and duties of subjects or citizens in their function as political beings. Charters and bills and declarations of rights abound in Western history. The Universal Declaration of Human Rights adopted by the United Nations in 1948 is in some respects the most significant action ever taken by a world organization, not because of its obviously negligible practical effect, but because it represents a will—however feeble and imperfect—to replace the laws of nations with a law for all mankind. It has dealt a psychospiritual blow to tribalism. Like all such declarations, it is brittle and formalistic, but the Universal Declaration of Human Rights, far more than the United Nations itself, foreshadows the City of Man.

Our commonwealth must have a fundamental law setting forth the rights and responsibilities of citizenship, although perhaps we shall find a better instrument than a declaration formulated in Anglo-Roman legalese. The fundamental world law of citizenship will be a religious document: a pledge by society to the service of being. It will become our Ten Commandments, our Vinaya-pitaka, our Beatitudes.

The world law will quite possibly begin with the Kantian imperative, from which all responsibilities and rights of citizenship flow, that each member of the world community assumes an absolute obligation to treat his fellow men as ends in themselves. The essence of community is reciprocity, mutuality, fellowship. No man exists for another, but all men, as citizens of a commonwealth, agree to seek their common weal, respecting the dignity of personhood and the dignity of mankind. As soon as some men fall to the subhuman level of serving as the implements of other men, the community is threatened with dissolution. In this sense, true communities have seldom existed since the beginning of civilization.

From the imperative to treat others as ends in themselves follows the responsibility of all world citizens not to injure, defraud, enslave, or exploit their fellow citizens. Some forms of injury, fraud, enslavement, and exploitation are impossible to measure or prevent, but the world law can lay down guidelines for dealing with the rest. Present legislation in most countries is especially defective in its approach to exploitation. Given the legitimate demands of a large world population on the material resources of the planet, our commonwealth will prohibit net personal incomes more than four times greater than the guaranteed universal basic income. Any surplus earned will be taxed at the rate of one hundred percent.

World citizens will also accept positive responsibilities. They will acknowledge an obligation to their children, to ensure their welfare during their minority, whatever form of family life the parents choose, and regardless of how much or how little help in child rearing they receive from the schools of the commonwealth. World citizens will have a direct obligation to the commonwealth itself, to provide for the maintenance of its institutions, through the payment of a progressive income tax and through acceptance of conscription for limited periods of time in the world army if its professional troops need reinforcements or in world service forces required to perform vital public work when normal means of recruitment fail.

No less important, every world citizen will owe to himself and his fellow citizens respect for the natural environment they share together. In a world of twelve billion human beings, respect for the environment means not only the avoidance of waste and needless pollution of air, earth, and water; it means the limitation of any parent to two children, and if such restraint is not forthcoming voluntarily, it must be required by law. The right to reproduce is indeed sacred—but not when it denies to those already born the right to live.

Of all the privileges of citizenship in the world commonwealth, the "right to live" must be deemed the most fundamental. Following Locke and Jefferson, the Universal Declaration of Human Rights guarantees "life, liberty and security of person," but the right to live involves more than the right of life. To live, for a man, is to fulfill as far as possible the potentialities of his being. I take as my model neither Locke, nor Jefferson, nor the Universal Declaration, but the first article of the Sankey Declaration of the Rights of Man, drafted during the Second World War in Great Britain by a committee whose moving spirit was H. G. Wells. "Every man," the first article affirmed, "is a joint inheritor of all the natural resources and of the powers, inventions and possibilities accumulated by our forerunners. He is entitled, within the measure of these resources . . . to the nourishment, covering and medical care needed to realize his full possibilities of physical and mental development from birth to death."

These are hard words for believers in the bourgeois ethic of work and the doctrine of the survival of the fittest. They are equally hard words for the less developed countries of our own time, whether socialist or capitalist, who can barely feed their workers, let alone the unemployed. But in a fully developed and socialized world economy, mankind will be able to offer all its citizens an income sufficient for their fundamental needs, without obligation to work at all. Every adult will earn, by right as a citizen, a minimum guaranteed wage, even if he does nothing more with his life than eat and sleep. The guardians of children will also receive a grant for each child in their care; the amount of the grant will increase as the child grows older. Nearly everyone, I am confident, will engage in work of various kinds in spite of the assurance of a decent minimum income: to earn extra money, to fulfill personal ambitions, to escape boredom, and to serve being. But the crucial point is that no community capable of caring for all its members can let even one of them suffer needlessly. The dignity of a fellow human being does not depend upon his "productiveness." Dignity is inherent and inalienable.

With the right to live must come the right to education, as discussed in Chapter Six. In some ways, the two rights are the same, since for *Homo sapiens* living is inseparable from learning, and self-fulfillment is impossible without acquiring some of the skills and knowledge of human culture. As we have defined work, the right to education is also, in great measure, the right to work.

But there are other kinds of work, and the right to all that are nonexploitative must be protected by the world law. The right to work will include the right of enterprise, the proprietorship of private venture capital in certain clearly delimited fields of economic activity, which we shall describe in the next section of this chapter. Even a socialist commonwealth can gladly grant the right of enterprise, for enterprise is one of mankind's historic modes of personal fulfillment. Only when the entrepreneur uses his capital to own other men, to deprive them of their fair earnings, and to take more than his own share of the world's wealth, does he become an enemy of society. In the world commonwealth, entrepreneurs will be limited to the same maximum personal income as anyone else, and they will be restrained by both moral and legal bonds from exploiting their fellow citizens.

Lastly, the world law of citizenship will guarantee to all persons the basic civic and political liberties of a free society. Some of these no longer need explanation or defense. Most nations today commit themselves to protect freedom of peaceful assembly, conscience, speech, publication, and artistic expression. Most decree freedom from public discrimination on the basis of race, nationality, religion, sex, class, or birth. The right to the equal protection of the laws, due process, the franchise, and participation in government is well established. No nation on earth has created conditions in which all these liberties are in fact enjoyed by all its citizens. Terrifying countertendencies threaten to negate the progress already made.

But at the level of ideas, civil libertarianism has done surprisingly well in the modern world, and the world law will strive to make its first triumphs permanent and irreversible.

But other basic freedoms remain largely unrecognized, even by liberals, and are still denied by the laws of many nations. Some we have discussed in Chapter Five. What of sexual rights? Freedom for group marriage? Freedom for homosexuality? The proprietorship of one's own body, including the right to use stimulants and psychedelic drugs? The right to abortion, sterilization, contraception, and euthanasia? The world law will guarantee to all its citizens full freedom of consensual erotic life. It will permit any responsible form of marriage and force no man or woman to live or reproduce against his will. It will place no bar upon any kind of private sensory experience, and it will "protect" no sane adult citizen against himself by means of legislation.

Further: no citizen of the world commonwealth will be subject to judicial punishment for violation of any law. Since punishment, whether in the form of execution, torture, imprisonment, or fines, has had a proven insufficient deterrent effect upon criminal behavior, and breeds inhumanity both in the punishers and in the punished, our commonwealth will renounce its use categorically. It will acknowledge that crimes against society are the result of psychological or social disorder, and that offenders can best be deterred from committing future crimes by undergoing a program of rehabilitative therapy.

The main reason that such programs are so rare in the modern world is their cost. The world civilization, with its great numbers of trained professional men and women, and its radically different postindustrial economic structure, will have far more time to spare the sick and the maladjusted. Offenders will be treated much like medical patients, living at home or in clinics under the care of specially trained psychiatrists and counsellors. The state will abandon its traditional role of avenging angel, and all Bastilles will fall at last.

In these and other ways the world civilization will do its best to counter the forces that militate against freedom inherent in the logic of technique and in the animal origins of human nature. I do not expect our efforts to prove entirely successful. No matter how skillfully we write our laws, no matter how much influence our religion and ethical culture may exert, the demands of a mass order dependent on technology will take their toll. In these later chapters, I have sometimes had to recommend technical solutions not very different from those that in Chapter One I attacked the nation-states for using. Nor can I reasonably hope that men in the world civilization will always be able to resist the temptation to exploit other men. The instinct of self-preservation has a natural inclination to work overtime. But the fundamental law of the world civilization must set severe limits on every application of technical logic that tends to curtail freedom. It must be liberal and liberating to the furthest bounds of the possible. If we do not resolve to make it so, our struggle to achieve world integration loses all human meaning.

4. Welfare

Economic historians and futurologists have acquainted us in recent years with the imminence of a great change in the economic life of mankind. Although some societies have yet to leave the Stone Age, others are evolving from industrial to postindustrial economies, to a stage of development quite different from the industrialism of the nineteenth and twentieth centuries. The manufacturing industries absorb relatively less labor, capital, and entrepreneurial energy, while the service industries (including government) and the professions absorb relatively more. This change in emphasis is certain to increase steadily in the last decades of the twentieth century. It now seems equally certain that, if events take their natural course, only a small number of societies can ever make the transition to a fully postindustrial economy. The others will be left gasping for breath at various earlier stages along the way, defeated by population pressures, lack of education and capital, feudalism, inequitable distribution of purchasing power, neocolonialism, and the greater ability of the developed countries to cope with ecological deterioration.

Such a prospect is unacceptable, for political as well as humanitarian reasons. The goal of the world commonwealth must clearly be an integrated world economy in which all segments of mankind prosper equally. But the world commonwealth will not have the option of achieving this goal by reversing the historic trend toward postindustrialism. A stabilization of the world economy at the level of Great Britain *circa* 1830 or the Han Dynasty *circa* 100 A.D. is unthinkable. Stages must be overleaped, development must be artificially stimulated and controlled, and consumption patterns must be altered to make possible the entrance of all mankind into the postindustrial era before the end of the twenty-first century. Such a feat is entirely within our power, given the emergence of a new civilization with a new ethical culture, and the establishment of a world commonwealth.

A postindustrial world civilization will also be, to a great extent, a posteconomic civilization. As with government, so with economics: both will tend to recede into the background of human life, despite their continuing practical importance. A variety of contrasts come to mind, which reveal the curve of change. Traditional man sought a stable economic order but accepted vast extremes of wealth and poverty; industrial man sought infinite economic growth and reduced substantially the gap between rich and poor; posteconomic man will seek to combine stability with modest growth (if any) and will build an essentially classless society. Traditional man believed in the highest possible birth rate, to ensure a plentiful supply of hands and wombs; industrial man practiced a certain amount of birth control, but saw gradual demographic growth as an index of progress; posteconomic man will attempt to reduce the world's population by lowering the birth rate drastically. Traditional man worked to survive; industrial man worked, early in his history, to maximize production and, later, to maximize consumption; posteconomic man will work to achieve personal growth.

One thing alone will make a posteconomic society possible: the logic of technique, carried one step further than it has ever been carried before. In the industrial society, machines took over much of the labor once performed only by men and animals. Every aspect of the economic process was subjected to intensive rationalization. But in the posteconomic society, technique will facilitate the full automation of agriculture and industry, and machines will do virtually all the work, both mental and physical, that men choose not to do. Such a development need not in itself contribute to the further dehumanization of society. On the contrary, it will encourage rehumanization, since it will tend to remove human beings from the economic process altogether, freeing them from enslavement to the rhythm of the machine, and giving them time to pursue humanizing work at their own tempo and pleasure. It is not technique itself that dehumanizes man, but rather the necessity, in a precybernetic technology, to convert human beings into the eyes and ears and brains of mechanical bodies, or of machine-like economic organizations. In such imperfect circumstances, human beings become in effect "cyborgs," half-human, half-mechanical. Sever the wires that connect flesh and metal, and the flesh is free. Or, let us say, more free than before. Obviously the logic of technique has more power over mankind than it exerts in the economic process.

But we shall all be more free and the quality of life will rise in a post-industrial economy. Such an economy is well worth achieving. It will also render somewhat easier the solution of the other basic economic problems confronting mankind in its search for world order. We may reduce these to three: the problem of the rich and poor nations, the problem of the exhaustion of the environment, and the problem of the ownership of the means of production.

I have already cited some of the reasons for the steady worsening of the economic disparity between the technologically advanced and the technologically backward countries in the twentieth-century world. Every attempted remedy fails—even when it seems to succeed. The loans and technical assistance offered unilaterally by the advanced countries have tended only to strengthen the hand of existing regimes, most of which follow social policies that retard economic development. Investment by the private corporations of the advanced countries typically works to the advantage of the investors and a few members of local elites, leaving the mass of the people untouched. Efforts at cooperation and mutual aid among the poor nations are seldom of much value, since their economies are too primitive to interact vigorously, and political rivalry stemming from neonationalism generates distrust.

The only stratagem that has worked at all is self-help, the adoption of a rigorous policy of national regeneration, usually preceded by a political revolution of some kind. Japan and Soviet Russia have both, in very different ways, lifted themselves out of preindustrial poverty in a relatively short span of time, with little outside assistance. Maoist China seems well on her way to the same goal.

The price exacted by this rapid progress is prohibitively high. Fanatical social-revolutionary discipline nourishes, and in turn is nourished by xenophobia and imperialistic nationalism. The growth of personal freedom is stunted. The benefits of economic specialization are sacrificed for the short-term security of national economic self-sufficiency, a goal unattainable by small nations, and inimical to the greater goal of world integration. Nevertheless, some non-Western countries have succeeded in emulating the economic development of the West without help and without following a slow historic process of industrial evolution on the Western model.

But the lesson of their success (if it should be called success) is not that self-help alone saves a country from poverty, or that outside interference and aid are fatal to economic growth. The crucial factor has been the awakening of a sense of community. The sense of togetherness instilled by nationalism encourages people to work as one to achieve national objectives. Where this feeling is not sufficiently developed, as in Afghanistan or India, growth is inadequate, despite outside aid. Where social discipline is strong, a region such as Soviet Uzbekistan—an Asian nation in its own right, with a distinctive culture, and a prerevolutionary economic level similar to that of Afghanistan—can benefit from outside (chiefly Russian) help and advance rapidly. The same is true of relatively backward regions in the United States, which national assistance may have saved from perennial stagnation or even collapse.

In the coming world civilization, we shall have both the sense of community and whatever outside aid is needed to bring every region up to the planetary average. The postindustrial regions will curtail their domestic consumption in order to supply capital for swift development elsewhere. The industrial phase may be bypassed altogether in many poorer regions, which will leap directly from a basically traditional agrarian economy to postindustrial automation. Wherever a man is born, he will enjoy the same opportunities for fulfillment, as the heir not only of the common world culture, but also of the same worldwide community of wealth.

I would also expect considerable regional economic specialization in the new society. In an equalized world where no region has cause to fear aggression or exploitation by another, and tariff walls have all disappeared, each region will be free to concentrate on the sort of agriculture, mining, manufacturing, and services that best suit its natural resources. Trade from region to region will be brisk. All this will have only a limited effect upon the populations of each region, since self-regulating, self-maintaining machines will do most of the actual work, but it will increase by a measurable percentage the world's wealth.

Yet I should not give the impression that our "community of wealth" will be a world swimming in opulence of the kind already familiar to millions of upper-strata families in the developed countries. On the contrary. By the standards of these privileged few, the world way of life will seem austere, even monastic. We have argued in Chapter One that the most affluent portions of humanity are spending and fouling the earth's abundance like rats let loose in a granary. The imminent exhaustion of the envi-

ronment is the second great economic problem that the world commonwealth must solve, and it can do so only by careful husbanding and the
imposition of strict limits on personal income and the ancient right to reproduce.

As a matter of common justice and plain arithmetic, the greatest burden
will fall upon the developed countries. It will not seem as great a burden to
a mundialized nation sharing in the new world culture, as it would to the
same nation faced with the same prospect in the 1970's, but the sacrifices
will be difficult to make all the same. For more than a century, real personal incomes have risen steadily throughout the Western world. In the
world civilization, for many decades if not considerably longer, these incomes will not continue to rise; they will not level off; they will have to
drop precipitously.

There is no other way. If the billions of people now mired in profound
poverty are to experience even a modest increase in personal income, and
if the human race is to strike a reasonable natural balance with its environment, the consumption patterns of the rich must change completely. We
who find it "difficult" to exist today on a per capita annual income of several thousand dollars, will have to learn to make do on considerably less
than one thousand.

In this matter of the ecological balance, the citizens of the world commonwealth will submit—I should like to think almost cheerfully—to the
dictates of technique. By the twenty-first century, in any case, they will see
very little choice. Failure to institute world ecological planning and a system of world redistribution and rationing of vital raw materials will lead
infallibly to the end of all civilized life on earth, through war, famine, disease, and the total collapse of every economic system more advanced than
the Neolithic.

In a world civilization committed to rational solutions of the ecological
crisis, the imagination of men such as Buckminster Fuller will at last come
into its own. We shall need computer centers capable of assimilating and
correlating all the data we can supply them. We shall need to know how
fast we can afford to spend what is left, and how much we can allow each
region and each citizen. We shall learn how to make the most of what we
have, and how many children we can feed and rear.

I do not know what answers the computers will print out. But I do know
that for a world population of twelve billion, even if we manage by strenuous planning to bring it down to eight or four billion in the still more dis-

tant future, the earth will be hard pressed to yield more than a meager livelihood. We may learn eventually to eliminate pollution, tap the limitless energy of the sun, wring the minerals we need from rocks and sea water, nourish the multitudes with algae, transmute elements at will, and much more; but technological progress takes time, and just to keep pace with the population rise that is already more or less inevitable will probably strain our ingenuity to the full. To this task we cannot add the still bigger task of engineering a massive escalation of the living standards of the poor nations without correspondingly massive sacrifices by the rich.

The rich today have hardly begun to think of such things. Capitalist and socialist countries in the industrial stage think of nothing but economic growth leading to ever-rising levels of consumption. If they worry at all about what they use up or pollute in the process of moving larger and larger quantities of goods into more and more hands, it is only because they fear that something may happen to diminish, even temporarily, this mighty flow of goods. Measures to counteract soil erosion or depletion of minerals or poisoning of rivers and lakes are aimed at the immediate restoration of the flow at any cost.

But with changes in the mental climate, and above all a change in values, the passion to consume will cool, and the rich may become just as resourceful in finding ways of spending less as they are today in finding ways of spending more. In capitalist countries, an obvious place to begin is the winding down of the advertising industry, with its genius for persuading people to buy what they neither want nor need. We must also abolish the practice of producing goods that self-destruct after a few weeks or months in preference to durable ones that last five times as long at a marginally higher (and sometimes lower) cost to the producer. An equivalent vice in communist countries is the bureaucratically imposed production quota, which measures the worth of an industrial facility by its statistical output, with little regard to quality, consumer demand, ecological wastage, or long-range social value.

In every area of high-level consumption, except the consumption of services, the affluent classes and societies can make far-reaching cuts with little deleterious effect on the quality of life—often with an improving effect. Public rail transport systems, for example, must entirely replace the private automobile with its prohibitive costs of production and maintenance, its inefficient use of fuel, its pollutants, and its insatiable passion for burying the countryside under concrete. For short trips, bicycles (not to mention legs) will serve quite well. The detached private house will disappear, in favor of apartment buildings, large communal dwellings for the new forms of family life, and tent towns in warm climates, all furnished with extensive shared facilities, including sporting equipment, tools, cameras, tape recorders, musical instruments, and books and recordings.

The affluent can also contrive with little difficulty to spend much less on clothing and food than they do today. Modern technology has the capacity to manufacture attractive clothing that will far outwear almost anything mass-produced at the present time. Everyone will have a few changes of good clothes, and no more. They will eat vegetables, fruits, whole grain cereals, and perhaps a little cheese and fish, instead of the costly meats and processed "delicacies" that send grocery bills into the stratosphere today. Of alcoholic beverages, all but the most inexpensive locally produced beers and wines will vanish from the market, or carry prices so high that no one can afford to buy them except for very special occasions.

Schools and universities, although greatly increased in number, will cost less to build and operate in the future world society than they do today. I see them as quite modest in size, with many and perhaps most class meetings conducted informally outdoors, in the homes of teachers, or in multipurpose public buildings. Universities will bear little resemblance to Oxford or Yale. With few exceptions, students will live at home and commute to the campus, or to their instructors' homes. Libraries will be quite small, since nearly all materials will be stored on microforms. As far as possible, the academy will return to its simple Platonic beginnings. Only fields such as the natural sciences, engineering, and medicine will require elaborate facilities.

The automation or liquidation of most office work will also spare the economy the necessity of constructing endless numbers of great office buildings. Computers can be housed more cheaply than clerks and secretaries and vice-presidents. The reduction of armies to a single small world peace-keeping force will free immense resources now squandered on military bases and equipment. We shall have no prisons, no millionaires, no newspapers and magazines swollen to three times their proper size by advertisements; no stock markets, no automobile showrooms, no expensive generalissimos and sheikhs.

I grant that some of these things will be missed. But we shall be more than compensated for our losses even in a purely economic sense by the expansion and improvement of services of every kind. There will be more

and better teachers, artists, dancers, musicians, doctors, dentists, professional athletes, craftsmen, tailors, repairmen, barbers, therapists, social
workers, clergymen, public speakers, writers, actors, even prostitutes (if we
need them). Whatever people—as opposed to material goods—can do to
make our lives richer, will be done.

Nor should we overlook the many good things in life that we can do for
ourselves without the spending of a penny. The goal for the men and
women of the foreseeable future, as John Kenneth Galbraith urged in a recent interview with Frances Cairncross of *The Observer*, is "not consumption, but the use and enjoyment of life." The tendency to associate happiness with expenditure, he adds, is a bad habit acquired from economics
textbooks. "In a rational life style, some people could find contentment
working moderately and then sitting by the street—and talking, thinking,
drawing, painting, scribbling, or making love in a suitably discreet way.
None of these requires an expanding economy." The age of "persuaded
and competitive consumption," the age of the lemming-man who spends
all his days in the marketplace ferociously acquiring an income that he
lacks the leisure or the culture to enjoy, begins already to seem obsolete.
"Once a Cadillac has come to look comic, it never looks any other way. Or
a dull suburban house. Once people discover that they are enslaved by
their consumption—and the advertisers—they seek emancipation, and for
good."

Assuming that Galbraith is right, we are left with only one question to
answer in this survey of welfare in the world society. Who will own the
means of production? Will the world economy be socialist or capitalist?

We have already answered this question in the most direct way: it will
be socialist. But this is not a full answer. I am not a doctrinaire socialist,
and I have no objection in principle to private enterprise. But there is all
the difference in the world between the entrepreneur who risks his savings,
and those of his companions, to try some new way of producing or selling
goods or services, and the vulpine corporate manipulator who plays with
billions of dollars and strives for the oligopolistic control of his market with
one or two other equally vulpine "competitors." The oligopolist (or mo-
nopolist—it is all the same) is no longer primarily an entrepreneur: he
wields public power, as if he were a minister of state or a commissar. Phenomena such as Howard Hughes and Aristotle Onassis bear living witness
to sociopathogenic forces in capitalism no less virulent than the forces that
produced, in the communist world, the figure of Joseph Stalin.

But whether one thinks of the great foxes of capitalism, or the smaller fry in dark suits who collectively dispose of even greater wealth and power, the picture is much the same. The corporation is not private enterprise. It buys and sells whole nations; it corrupts the marketplace and strangles true competition; its owners and managers take far more from society than they can possibly give in return. In its time, it was one way of promoting rapid economic growth; Marx saw capitalism as a necessary historic evil. But as Marx also prophesied, capitalism invariably reaches an evolutionary cul-de-sac. It becomes monopolistic. It becomes an end in itself.

Unhappily, the dialectical opposite of capitalism—modern communism —has also failed to fulfill its early promise, if the Soviet experience is any guide. Whether capital is owned by plutocrats or held in perpetual trust by the state, gross inequalities in income persist, the environment is despoiled, and men lose their souls in huge dehumanized corporate-bureaucratic labyrinths. It remains to be seen whether China can avoid traveling the same road already taken by the Soviets.

The world commonwealth can do better. It will combine the best features of both capitalism and socialism, in a predominantly socialist framework, relying on the progress of automation to negate the dehumanizing impact of industrial giantism. Since most corporations are in effect no longer competitive or private, except in ownership, the commonwealth will convert all but the smallest factories, mines, plantations, banks, insurance companies, retail chain stores, and the like into public property, under the control of state corporations directed by the ministry of welfare. All utilities and transport systems, wherever they remain in private hands, will undergo the same conversion. Socialization of private corporations may result in a decline in the inventiveness of industry, although every state enterprise will maintain research facilities. But our goal, very clearly, is not headlong economic growth. We shall not miss the deluge of new products and new models of old products continuously dumped on the market today. Our first concern will be to ensure the survival of mankind and of civilization by developing a stable, planned, conserving, equalitarian, and humane economic order. If this means a rate of economic development more like the medieval rate than the modern, no one will lose any sleep over it.

At the same time, it should be possible to save some space in the economy for authentically private enterprise. The right of enterprise is one of the privileges of citizenship in the world commonwealth discussed in the preceding section, and a privilege that I think will be vigorously exercised by many men and women in the future society. Entrepreneurs in this new society may be single individuals, a small consortium of individuals pooling their savings, or a cooperative association with hundreds or thousands of members. Under appropriate circumstances, loans will be made to entrepreneurs by state banks, religious bodies, or other public or private organizations having capital resources.

A common form of entrepreneurial activity will be the craftsman's shop, where goods of high quality are produced by one or more skilled artisans to respond to needs—primarily aesthetic—that cannot be met by the merchandise of automated factories. Other shops will be established to manufacture experimental products, which may become successful enough that the world commonwealth will wish to buy the patent and mass-produce them. In some private businesses, clothes will be styled to order by expert tailors, or shoes and boots by expert cobblers. The demand for such things will be quite limited, given the relatively low purchasing power of every consumer, but those who value handcrafted goods should have the chance to buy them.

Many other types of private enterprise can be foreseen. Small farms will specialize in growing unusual fruits and vegetables. Private restaurants will provide occasional respite from home or institutional cooking. Private publishers will give authors an alternative to publication by state or university presses. Many services will be marketed by private entrepreneurs. Although all medical and most legal services will be paid for by public insurance, a substantial proportion of doctors and lawyers will no doubt maintain their own offices instead of working as employees of state institutions. There will be private schools and universities, beauty and barber shops, bazaars, sports clubs, taverns, theaters, and much more.

But there will be no enterprise of any kind for the sake of exploitative profit. As we pointed out earlier, the personal income of any citizen will not exceed four times the universal minimum wage. However successful the entrepreneur may be in his work, he cannot earn more than four times as much as if he did nothing at all. This may eliminate the incentive to do well for some people, but given the new attitude to work of the world culture, given its definition of work as growth, I think the absence of opportunity for unlimited personal gain will matter little. Even for the entirely materialistic personality, the chance to earn three or four times the minimum wage will provide just as much incentive as the chance to earn three or four hundred times the average income in the world of today. If no citizen can make more than a fixed amount, there will be no "higher" goal to aim for. What is fair and tolerable for all will be fair and tolerable for each.

Although I can do no more than guess, it seems plausible to imagine twenty-five percent of the world's adult population engaged in private enterprise of one kind or another. Fifty percent will be employed as teachers, students, and research scholars and resident artists in the educational system (including the relatively small number of persons in private schools and universities). Ten percent will work in government, apart from education, as statesmen, judges, ministry and public corporation staff employees, soldiers, lawyers, architects, physicians and nurses at public hospitals and clinics, and so forth. The rest of the world's people will freely elect to do nothing except live. In case of some great planetary emergency, where manpower is vitally needed, they will be subject to conscription into special military or labor forces, but no more so than any other citizen.

Having tried to envision how people will live in the world commonwealth, let us now explore briefly the question of where they will live.

5. The Future of the City

Western man has periodically, since the early nineteenth century, experienced pangs of regret for a hypothetical order of unsullied nature that he saw retreating before the steady march of industrial civilization. We are in the middle of such a mood of reaction in the early 1970's. The model for living of a broad segment of the neoromantic counterculture is a small colony in the wilderness, surrounded by snowy mountains, turquoise lakes, and forests thick with game and songbirds. The people of the colony raise their own organically grown foods, bake their own bread, and sing folk ballads in the evening by the fireside.

I cannot paint such splendid pictures of life in the coming world civilization. If everyone chose to form small colonies in the wilderness, and if they razed every city and suburb and factory to create additional wilderness, the planet would still have room for no more than five percent of the people who now inhabit it, and a much smaller percentage of the people who will inhabit it by the year 2050. The vision of a new Eden is a dream that can never come true, until most of mankind migrates to the stars, or dies.

Nevertheless, the neoromantics are on the right track, as are the Chinese, whose leaders have apparently managed to arrest the drift of popula-

tions to the cities in recent years, and whose current official doctrine calls
for rural self-reliance and the prevention of megalopolitan sprawl.
Throughout most of the rest of the world, urban areas grow inexorably.
Inner cities are fed by a never-ending stream of rural poor in search of
work. The outer cities, replete with residential suburbs, attract most of the
wealth of every nation. Unlike battleships, which they much resemble, skyscrapers are still being built in large numbers. Despite overcrowding, inadequate transportation systems, air pollution, strikes, slums, and all the
other miseries of urban existence, the cities continue to grow. A few, such
as London and Paris, are still the most stimulating places in the world to
make one's home.

But the ascendancy of the cities will not continue forever. On the contrary, I foresee the relative decline of urban agglomerations in the world
society, and a radical decentralization of both industry and culture. The
very growth of the cities will end them: as each city reaches out to connect
with its neighbors, it spreads ever more thinly through the countryside,
while its core areas perceptibly deteriorate. In time, the city no longer exists as such. In its stead lies a patchwork of urban, suburban, and rural living spaces, weakly attached (if at all) to the urban core. When most of the
work of industry and government is automated, and universities and other
local cultural centers realize their full potential, the original nuclear city
will have lost its reason for being. Mankind will tire of the city. Its towers
will be pulled down, or preserved as museums.

Most of these great transformations are already beginning to happen, for
those who have eyes to see. Factories and offices have been relocating in
suburban areas and small towns for many years in the Western world, although not rapidly enough to halt the growth of the cities. Anyone familiar
with the campus life of American universities situated in "college towns,"
such as Princeton, Michigan, and Stanford, will appreciate the extent to
which a thriving academic community can recreate most of the attractions
of urban higher culture, with none of its inconveniences. Still more re-
markable, much the same sort of thing occurs on far less celebrated campuses, located at greater distances from major urban centers.

In the world commonwealth, the mission of urban life, characterized by
Lewis Mumford as the furthering of "man's conscious participation in the
cosmic and the historic process" and the "magnification of all the dimensions of life," will be taken up by every village and commune and town

and region of the whole globe. We shall not need cities, because the world will become a single City of Man, a cosmopolis from end to end.

The most visible change will be the transfer of manufacturing installations, power plants, agricultural plantations, and government computer centers to industrial parks, staffed by small residential crews of supervisors and technicians. Apart from these crews, such parks will have no human inhabitants at all. A great network of railways, pipelines, and cables will connect them to one another and to the outside world, but they will certainly not be classifiable as cities.

The ministries of welfare and ecology will set aside other parts of the earth as wilderness reservations, somewhat like the national parks of the North American Far West, where men and women and children can come to hike, camp, boat, fish, ski, climb mountains, and observe wild life. Even on the most crowded of planets, there will still be small uninhabited islands and patches of desert, jungle, high country, arctic wasteland, and forest suitable for adventuring, although only a small fraction of the population will be able to visit them at any one time, and trips will have to be carefully rationed.

But the center of life, I suspect, will become the small town, of five or fifteen or twenty-five thousand people, with its college and university, its small local shops, as well as state department stores, and its abundant public and private services. There will be great numbers of such towns. A world population of twelve billion could fill eight hundred thousand towns, each of fifteen thousand people; but since several moderately large metropolitan areas will probably survive, and other people will live in villages or industrial parks, the number of towns might be closer to five hundred thousand, some old, some new, some carved from the suburbs and quarters of extinct cities. Not all towns will be able to have universities of their own, but all will be situated within a few miles of one, and will take ready advantage of its facilities.

We described the university in Chapter Six as a complex cultural center, with a staff consisting not only of scholars and teachers, but of men and women in almost every field of cultural endeavor. Artists, musicians, actors, dancers, and writers in residence will enrich the life of the whole town with their exhibitions and performances. As less emphasis comes to fall on the mawkishly overpublicized megalopolitan "star" and more local talent is identified and brought to fruition by an incomparably better system of education, we shall discover what some of us have suspected for a long time, that there are hundreds of thousands of Goyas, Schuberts, Bernhardts, Nijinskys, and Balzacs in the world, waiting to bloom in the sunlight of public recognition. Some talents will still surpass others, and the peculiar combination of luck and ability that leads to world fame will still elude most. But the notion of the absolutely transcendent and superhuman genius is a romantic myth. Instead of the same few hundred certified geniuses occupying center stage in a few megalopolitan centers before the same few thousand certified connoisseurs, we shall have a world brimming with talent, and a broad public well enough educated to appreciate and applaud what talent can do.

Not that everyone will be a producer or patron of the arts. Community sporting clubs will compete against one another in great numbers and variety, with the enthusiasm nowadays largely reserved for the most affluent big-city teams. There will be circuses, public dances, festivals, religious ceremonies, sacred orgies, and many forms of communal celebration still unthought of. Town meetings will discuss the great issues of the day. University scholars will offer frequent public lectures, and one-seventh of all adult citizens in any one year will be taking sabbatical leaves at colleges or universities in the region. Books, magazines, microform libraries, television, films, and inexpensive rapid public transport systems will link each town to the larger world outside.

These will be no bumpkins, these townsmen of the world civilization. Like the citizens of the ancient Greek *poleis* or the burghers of the imperial free towns of old Germany or the self-reliant villagers of colonial New England, they will bear comparison with any men of their time. On a densely settled planet, town life will offer a sense of space and freedom that our urban agglomerations of today too often crush.

CHAPTER EIGHT

Cosmos

1. Man and Nature

After composing my picture of the world commonwealth, this unheroic beehive if you please, this prosaic paradise of philandering scholars and gentle craftsmen bending over their workbenches, this new Middle Age of serried little towns and ration books and birth quotas and humanistic popery, I hear my friend Friedrich Nietzsche groaning from his private hole in Hell. He recites a fragment of *The Will to Power*, section eight sixty-six. I have built in my imagination the society of his "first road," the road to

> adaptation, leveling, higher Chinadom, modesty in the instincts, satisfaction in the dwarfing of mankind—a kind of *stationary level of mankind*. Once we possess that common economic management of the earth that will soon be inevitable, mankind will be able to find its best meaning as a machine in the service of this economy—as a tremendous clockwork, composed of ever smaller, ever more subtly "adapted" gears; as an ever-growing superfluity of all dominating and commanding elements; as a whole of tremendous force, whose individual factors represent *minimal forces, minimal values.*

Is our cosmopolitan social democracy not the heat-death of mankind? Will it not damn us all to perpetual mediocrity? Must the human race fade into the mindless harmony of primeval nature?

Man and nature! Mysticism and Eastern thought discover their oneness. Nature is the eternal music to which man must attune his being. Judeo-

Christian and modern Western thought holds the opposite view: nature is given to man, for his joy and his progress. Let him bend nature to his divine will.

We have seized now on the final question for the City of Man, the challenge that determines whether it lives or dies. To serve being, shall we become obedient natural creatures, or shall we subdue nature to our arbitrarily chosen human purposes? When mankind has constructed its world civilization, what then?

Although it may seem impossibly abstruse, the problem of how man should relate his being to the larger being of nature is also deeply practical. We have examined it in the context of religion and moral philosophy, in Chapter Four. We have examined it in the context of world economic development, in Chapter Seven. Now let us anticipate the interaction of man and nature in the commonwealth of a more distant future, after our survival has been ensured, and terrestrial unity is the normal condition of *Homo sapiens*. Nietzsche's unhappy vision of a "higher Chinadom"—the whole world transformed into something like the decadent China of the later Ch'ing emperors—suggests one alternative. We may settle into a great autumnal age, melting into the natural order like a decomposing corpse. The romances of American science-fiction novelists furnish the model of another alternative future: interminable wars between the space fleets of rival galactic empires. The Faustian man of science fantasy is never satiated. Scorning the slumbers of lower nature, he must have more, and yet more life.

The choice of unending slavery or unending piracy is actually a false choice, between antithetical world views that are fully true only when they meet and fuse. Man is not a mushroom or a rabbit. He does not follow the deep subrational life of land and sea. Yet again, he is not alone in the cosmos: all that he is grows from the same world-stuff as everything else. He is, and he is not, a natural being. Every effort to derive a consistent code of life from the behavior of other species, peaceful or violent, stable or evolving, solitary or gregarious, collapses upon itself. Every effort to construct a morality that ignores the filial bonds between mankind and the cosmos, ends also in futility.

Thus at one pole sits the Buddha who pierces the veil of time and personhood, who sublimely abjures all striving and lets his being dissolve into the absolute suchness of eternity. At the other pole sits the modern philos-

opher pale with nausea at the sight of the swelling opacity of the world
outside personal existence, that being-in-itself which he can never penetrate, but which one day will engulf him in the meaningless vacuum of
death. Both experiences, the mystical and the antimystical, are true, and
untrue. We learn, and do not learn, from both.

The sane response is synthesis. Man must be himself, and for himself, in
the fullness of his being. The nature that he strives to obey must be his own
nature, as a child of eternal being who has, all the same, reached the age of
self-determination, and becomes in his life the cosmos made conscious.
Among the creatures of this earth, man alone is a reasoning, caring, planning, choosing, loving entity. He cannot disavow the sources of his being,
nor can he disavow his uniqueness. His ground in all reality is the older
truth; yet it is false, or at best incomplete, without the younger truth, that
nature has liberated him to shape himself, and that his freedom forces him
to act.

Toward nature, then, man must be reverent as to a father of ripe years,
and to his father's house and fields, and to all the surrounding warmth in
which he grows to manhood. He must conserve his inheritance, but he
must use it in wisdom for himself and his posterity. Because the future of
intelligent earthly life depends on him for all it can become, his higher
duty is to the future. Because he is a mere fever of willing without the past,
he cannot discharge that duty unless he also receives the blessings of his
heritage.

This is to ask the impossible, perhaps. To become simultaneously Gau-
tama and Jean-Paul Sartre—and also Jesus and Arthur Schopenhauer? Yet
I think mankind spirals toward such a consummation. Many of the great
forces now moving the mind of Eastern man are Western, from technocracy to Marxism; many of the great forces now moving the mind of Western man are Eastern, from yoga to Zen. We advance dialectically toward
the fuller truth of the coming world culture, toward a synthesis no less revolutionary than the synthesis that gave us civilization itself more than six
thousand years ago.

For the City of Man, this view of the relationship between man and nature issues in the judgment that the world civilization must be a world
order and also more than a world order. In its initial phase, which we have
dwelled upon in previous chapters, the new civilization will devote most of
its energies to the stabilization of human life. It will build a new order, in

place of the national orders. It will plan for unity, peace, equality, freedom, and conservation of the environment. It will save mankind from the suicidal recklessness of modern Western civilization.

The world society will never abandon its mission of world pacification, but in time it must lay equal emphasis upon quite a different goal: the enlargement of man's humanity. Perhaps we shall need a second revolution, to break loose from the austere mentality of the first generations of world leaders, schooled (as they must be) in the soldierly arts of survival. Yet just because those first leaders will have constructed a world order that also insists upon absolute freedom of thought and research, such a revolution should have little difficulty marshaling its forces and finding broad public support.

The "enlargement of humanity" will demand more than the protection of personal freedom, or the conservation of life. I see the world commonwealth, as early as its second century, actively engaged in promoting the full self-realization of the species through coordinated worldwide research and development projects. Far from resisting, it will encourage and perhaps even initiate powerfully innovative movements in cultural life. New sciences and technologies will spring into being; new forms and media of communication; new arts and crafts; new philosophies and religions. In due course, the advance of technical skill will permit the level of material prosperity enjoyed by today's affluent nations to return, if mankind still wants it, accompanied this time by infallible safeguards against ecocide. The world government, and its laws, will prove no less immune to change.

All this, in a sense, will constitute change for the sake of change or, let us say, change for the sake of giving young people the same opportunity their elders enjoyed to renew life on their own terms. Any system perpetuated for centuries, whether intrinsically good or bad, becomes bad if it becomes automatic, if it no longer engages the will, but requires only the skills of the faithful copyist.

At the same time, innovation will also facilitate, along certain lines of development, true human progress. Man will expand the qualities of his being that are quintessentially human. He may not be able to avoid repeating ancient errors, as he progresses. There may be new wars or famines or crimes against personhood. But some of his gains—in power, knowledge, wealth, skill, wisdom, goodness—will endure, and deepen his joy in himself and his love of being.

Most of the progress that the world society will make in its great days we cannot foresee, but one frontier stands open to view even in the 1970's. As an example of how man will seek self-enlargement, consider the implications of his newly acquired capabilities as a navigator of outer space.

2. The Migration to Heaven

One of the seven ministries of the world government mentioned in Chapter Seven was the ministry of space, but we gave it scant attention. The ecological crisis now in its opening phase will probably force the suspension of current national space programs long before the end of the century. We shall have all we can do to stay alive and work for world integration. I doubt if the world commonwealth will be able to resume mankind's systematic exploration of the solar system until many years after the revolution; even then, it may encounter the same kind of public resistance offered by the radicals and liberals who damn the American space effort today.

But the world commonwealth will elect, finally, to mount a very large program of space exploration. It will not begrudge the cost. In the end, the ministry of space may become the most important department of state.

We shall launch such a program for at least four reasons—two of them readily comprehensible in terms of the immediate needs of the world civilization, and two of them more difficult to explain, although they seem cogent enough to anyone who has taken the trouble to build his world view on the scale furnished by modern astronomy.

The first two reasons for a massive space program in the world civilization can be presented in a few words. The program will greatly increase our scientific knowledge of the universe, as the American and Soviet efforts have already begun to do; and the program will help prevent the petrifaction of the world order by supplying us with new challenges, new interests, new outlets for wanderlust, new ways of rechanneling man's instinctual aggressiveness. These are sober, present-minded reasons for exploring space. They apply equally well to our investigation of Antarctica, or the ocean floor, or the interior of the earth. The rewards are tangible. They begin with the first voyage.

But "space" is incomparably more vast than any little known feature of our own planet. It holds the moon and the eight sister planets of earth and their thirty satellites, some nearly as large as Mars. It holds the sun and all the stars of the Milky Way. By some estimates, our galaxy contains a stellar population of two hundred billion. If the Weizsäcker theory of planetary origins is correct, most of these stars support planetary systems of their own. But the galaxy itself has billions of sister galaxies, each with its billions of stars, and the universe continues, beyond the reach of our best instruments, worlds without end. Perhaps because we lack at present the technology required to travel farther than the inner planets of our own sun, we prefer not to think with any seriousness about the larger world to which our earth belongs. But I suspect it is nothing as rational as that. The full implications of the discoveries of astronomy have yet to pierce the deeper levels of our consciousness, and make contact with our feelings and imagination. The knowledge is too new. We feel more at ease with the wisdom of astrology—or tarot cards. We are still fewer than four centuries from the winter day in the year 1600 when Giordano Bruno was burned at the stake in Rome for teaching his doctrine of the infinity of worlds.

But Bruno was right, although he relied more on metaphysical speculation than on empirical science. The universe teems with stars and planets and moons, far more than we can now number. They exist in the same space-time continuum as earth. They are composed of the same matter and energy as we are, obeying the same natural laws. We know of nothing that prevents us from reaching out and touching them. No impassable locked gates or guardian monsters or force shields bar our way. We shall need to develop a more advanced technology, more powerful spaceships, methods for suspending animation during long flights; but the technological problems are almost certainly soluble. Given enough time, and enough explorers and way stations, the human race can eventually visit every solar system in the Milky Way. With still more sophisticated techniques, we can cross the intergalactic gulfs as well, although this would require us to find some way of evading the apparent physical impossibility of faster-than-light (ultraphotic) travel, or, alternately, of keeping the bodies of astronauts alive for hundreds of thousands of years.

But we shall do more than explore. I look on these deeps of outer space as the future homeland of most of the human race. I come now to the third reason for the decision by the world commonwealth to send expeditions to other parts of the cosmos: the imperative to serve being by fulfilling all the potentialities for life within our own beings. The same impulse that led us out of trees and caves, out of river valleys and nation-states, will lead us out of our native planet, to the universe beyond. Man will establish extraterrestrial colonies, adapting himself to conditions on new worlds, evolving into new races, creating new civilizations unlike any he has built on earth. If he is the cosmos made conscious, the instrument of being for its self-perception and self-enlargement, he cannot lie snug in his ancient nest forever. He has the obligation to spread his wings, and try the wind. Settling other worlds will also insure us—more effectively than any doomsday colony—against the possibility that human life may become extinct because of wars or natural disasters on the mother planet.

The enlargement of scientific knowledge, the provision of outlets for expansive energy, and man's duty to attain full realization of his being are three reasons, then, why the coming society will send its children into outer space. There is one other, and perhaps it is the most significant of all.

Earlier expeditions in human history led not only to the discovery of new land. They led also to the meeting of peoples previously unknown to one another. The interaction that ensued in the long run greatly enriched human culture. When mankind reaches the stars, it will certainly encounter other species of intelligent beings, some of them humanoid. If one star in a hundred is circled by a planet capable of supporting intelligent life, and intelligent life has actually evolved or will evolve on only one of every ten of these, our galaxy alone could give rise to two hundred million civilizations. A few will have reached the same approximate level of development as our own planetary society. Many will be much younger or older. The time for still others will not yet have come, or will have long since passed. Some of the living civilizations may also be exploring and colonizing their own galactic neighborhood.

We may assume that these fellow races will be scattered thinly through the cosmos, and that we shall not encounter one until we have been exploring for hundreds, perhaps thousands of years. We shall not attempt to colonize planets already inhabited by intelligent beings, but every effort will surely be made to establish diplomatic, economic, and cultural relations with any alien civilizations that we discover, or with any that discover us. The impact upon human life of close ties with a single extraterrestrial species could be immeasurably greater than that of any meeting of civilizations in man's history. What could a culture ten million years old teach us? Perhaps a culture only ten thousand years old could teach us more; but the possibilities are infinite. Even if we hypothesize that civilizations stop changing fundamentally after they reach a certain point of development not far beyond our own, contact with an alien culture only a little wiser or more powerful or more learned than earth's would still be a stimulating experience, and might set us upon new pathways of progress that we could not have found for ourselves.

Nor do meetings between civilizations necessarily occur only when both are alive: there is also the intertemporal contact, between a living society and a dead one. The dead society reaches across time through the records and artifacts it leaves behind, and may exert more influence upon the people who uncover its remains than they receive from neighboring societies of their own era. Western Europe during the Renaissance learned more from dead Hellenism than from living Islam. The same may happen in our exploration of outer space. Imagine the alien civilization which reached, by its own criteria, the summit of perfection, flourished at the summit for a million years, and then decided to submit to racial euthanasia. It passes away, but its well preserved bones—libraries, museums, cities—are discovered by earthmen, who in one stroke gain access to the accumulated wisdom of a society far greater than anything in terrestrial experience. It is conceivable that we may even find such a treasure trove on Mars. One such discovery would repay all the costs in lives and taxes of all the space programs that man could ever undertake.

Contact with alien species, as every reader of science-fiction knows, might also prove dangerous. Mankind could be exterminated or enslaved by a hostile advanced race. We might learn what would be better for us not to know. We might be tempted to embark on a program of conquest ourselves that would rehearse on a cosmic scale all the tragedies of the white imperialism of the nineteenth century. Or widely separated branches of the human race might build rival leagues in outer space that would eventually find themselves entangled in great internecine wars. The science-fiction novelists have no doubt already imagined most of the disasters that could occur.

But I think the world civilization will be prepared to take these risks. It will judge them worth taking, in light of all the potential benefits to mankind of space exploration. Its thinking men will appreciate, as most of us still do not, that we are natives not only of earth, but of all being. Although we may have a special historic claim upon this planet, in a deeper sense the whole cosmos belongs to us, and we to it. The service of being knows no frontiers, tribal or planetary. It is even possible that mankind may one day constitute a member race in a galactic union of intelligent species, a government of the cosmos, a republic of peoples pursuing a common destiny bound mind to mind and heart to heart. Such a union may already exist,

waiting to receive us when we have proved ourselves worthy of membership.

Clearly, almost anything is possible, in a nearly infinite universe.
Thought cannot reach far enough. But for this very reason we cannot turn
our faces to our terrestrial walls and refuse to hear the music of heaven. It
plays for all being, and a unified mankind will hear.

3. Songs in the Service of Being

In poetry we tell many discordant truths, not because we wish to deceive,
but because there are many truths. I have some poems about life, death,
man, nature, love. Mostly about love. Why we love being, how we feel
closed off from being, how we flow into it again, how we kill, how love is
misplaced, why worlds end.

We have just glanced at the prospect of galactic brotherhood. I begin
with seven questions. Three have never been asked before in the history of
literature.

> Could you love a long white worm
> Sleeping in his nest on Vega Five?
> Or nurse a broken trilobite
> Twitching in the thick primeval seas
> Of Sirius Three?
> What does it mean to love?
> Why should you celebrate the other life,
> The alien not-I,
> Why love a child, a girl, a wife?
> Why not the bullet
> Blown at your heart?
> Who loves a single other, but
> Cannot love the world?
> Is the golden sapient squid
> Composing odes on Aldebaran Six
> My fellow man?

Sometimes there is no brotherhood at all. Every nerve cries: There is no
being! Nothing but damned night, nothing but ice, and a thawing place
deep in the iceberg, where we hold a fellow sufferer close and try to stay
alive. Very true. Sometimes!

The world's not for seizing, holding, keeping
Just the way it was and is and will be.
None of it belongs to me.
But our molecules together
Make a moment's pause
In its continual shuttle back and forth
From alpha to omega.
None of it belongs to me,
None is yours, but for a moment we together
Lie commingling in its jaws.

Perhaps the cosmos has the same difficulty understanding man. So much variety, so many cross-purposes, so little communication! The vision of an inscrutable order of nature blind to our evil and our pain yields next to something warmer. The night bird was originally only a passing angel or a migrant hurrying on his way, but I wonder if he is not also a reconnaissance ship from the galactic federation, on the wing a thousand miles above Hiroshima?

The night bird, unblinking as the sun,
Flies fast, sings songs
Sweet and cool, flees the steaming ruins
On the land below.
He has his path to run,
And knows no tunes for man.
What would you, that a simple
Mindless bird should shed a feather,
Lose a moment's music, stop still-hearted
In mid-flight, to mourn for man?
Sometimes, for all that, he does.
The planets shudder in their courses
And the frame of things
Bends some degrees off plumb.
Then he must go on. Away with him,
The night bird flies like a devil,
Flings away all grief.
Stars roll. Skies turn.

At other times man and nature meet face to face. Here it happens in a boundary situation, where the land parts from the sea; and man sings the cosmic purpose.

> The song of long mornings
> Brought from gray and greenness
> By the burning of the sun
> Is sung most strongly
> By young men
> Whose sinewy throats the octaves
> In succession span.
> Let a choir gather by the shore
> Dressed in salted bronze,
> So the choir sings also bronzy hymns:
> In bass the thunderous deepness
> Of the sea, in baritone the burst
> Of waves flush on the beach,
> In tenor, monotone,
> The even growing of the morning
> Out at sea. Such hymns
> Outsoar the shrill white gull
> And fill the triton shell
> Tossed on the blinding sand.
> The morning lengthens, not brighter
> Or more bronze than singing men:
> Their song is stronger
> Than the ocean's antiphon.

Strophe, antistrophe. The choirs of civilization sing the cosmic purpose, but in reply the bombs of anticivilization split the sky. The twentieth century is like a lover's promise broken, a tryst not kept. We suffer more from disappointment than from dying.

> The sky smashed like a window
> Like the wife stoned for adultery
> Like the wandering Jew chased to the ends
> Of the un-mothering earth by blood-mad lambs.
> The rain came sharp and gleaming,

A rain of knives, and then the land—
The land cracked and heaved,
Boiled underfoot, we heard the sound—
The sound of sand becoming glass
The sound of men becoming grease
The sound of lovers finding
Loved ones faithless behind their faces:
The gift-box of the century unwrapped itself
But all it held was broken sky.

The problem of the twentieth century is not so much the absence of
love, as love misplaced. Love for idols. Stone idols in public parks, cloth
idols on poles, flesh idols in uniforms and ecclesiastical robes, idols of race
and blood and soil. I have invented an all-purpose tribal oath for idolaters.
Never read it except aloud, and every word must be screamed at the top of
your lungs.

I am black I am pink I am amber tan
I grew tall in the East in the West
In the South, my eyes are green
Are gray are brown, I love only my men
My girls my words my songs.
I march where my wind blows
I bloom where my grain grows
I shake my flag of blue of red
Of gold, great God for us,
And all for one!
To the end we run
We never will stop, we are black
We are pink we are amber tan
We are old we are young
We are long white sticks
We sprawl and shine in the sun.

The love that turns inward, the sense of the sacred that does not embrace all being, are ways of hating and profaning. Tribal society decorates
the xenophobic killer with medals and stones lovers who have no license
for the lawful breeding of future killers. Commonsense for the bull-ape in
his cave. Madness for us.

The old morality decrees that you and I
Mate like sun and sky, one sun, one sky.
But man is multitudes. Man is all the stars
Spinning in their trails.
The tribal law declares:
Each to his own! Buy one life
And dare not share! Fence your land! Freeze!
Each freshly planted suburb
Is a morgue of hearts.
But man is multitudes.
One day when we are free
To build cosmopolis,
The gay disease of love
Will take us all to bed,
One happy overflowing bed of lovers,
Free, free, free, great Zeus!
When shall we be free?

Now the complete dialectical truth about the future of mankind, in two songs. In the first, earth is a young love-child, hatched by the sun, and ready to take wing.

The lamps of knowing life
Burn starlike on sea-breasts
On jungle-tops in cloud-beds
Points banging points for joy.
Now Earth, the love-child,
Turns faster on her wheel.
Streams of solar mother's milk
Gave light and heat
She drank unendingly.
See how her skin begins to stir:
See living meteors
Threading the oceans of the sky.
Now the guardianship of our sun
Is nearly done.
Earth's egg-shell shakes
And breaks in two.

But in our last song, earth is an untended fireside, bleeding its heat into the sunset. Both images are true, as prospect. By our thought and action, we shall choose which becomes true. Great is truth, and it will prevail.

> How many years?
> Brothers hear me
> This one last time.
> We are dying, we people,
> The hearth of our home
> Cools. Our breath hangs gray
> And chill in the light of evening.
> We are dying,
> We people, hear me:
> How many years?
> Do you love the earth?
> Do you love the children?
> Do you love the grass
> The lizards the whales the wind rounding the rocks?
> Do you love lovers clasped for life's heat?
> How many years?
> All being cries to us,
> Shouts above our deafness:
> How many years?
> Think. Warm your wills. Strike.

Index

Academic freedom, 132–34
Aesop, 38
Affirmation, ethic of, 91–92
Afghanistan, 154
Albania, 58
Amalrik, Andrei, 15
Aquinas, St. Thomas, 135
Aristotle, 84, 135
Armstrong, Patrick, 35
Aron, Raymond, 5
Aurobindo, Sri, 51
Automation, 119–20, 152

Bahá'í faith, 56
Bahá'u'lláh, 56
Baldwin, Ian, Jr., 71
Barr, Stringfellow, 51
Baumer, Franklin L., 23
Bell, Daniel, 40
Benton, William, 34
Berr, Henri, 135
Bettelheim, Bruno, 104, 118
Bismarck, Otto von, 8
Boas, Franz, 34
Borgese, G. A., 51
Boulding, Kenneth, 36–37
Brameld, Theodore, 73, 124
Bruner, Jerome, 127
Bruno, Giordano, 170
Buddhism, 56, 82, 84, 166
Bultmann, Rudolf, 30, 55
Burma, 58

Canada, 42, 61
Capitalism, 3, 158–59
Ceylon, 58
China, 8, 15, 20, 41, 58, 64,
    78, 89, 104, 134, 153, 159,
    161, 166
Christianity, 49, 56, 90–91
Churchill, Winston S., 31
Cities, 161–64
Civil disobedience, 30–31, 44
Civilization, world, 27–29, 36,
    42, 46, 50–57, 77–173
Civil liberties, 149–50
Clark, Grenville, 51
Cognitive synthesis, 134–38
Collective security, 31–32
Colonies, for the renewal of
    civilization, 68–72; in outer
    space, 170–71
Comintern, 57
Commonwealth, world, 77,
    139–64
Communism, 159
Comte, Auguste, 9, 51, 56, 135,
    137
Condorcet, Marquis de, 51
Confucianism, 82
Congo, Republic of the, 58
Cosmopolitanism, 52–54
Cousins, Norman, 51
Cox, Harvey, 111
Crime and punishment, 150
Cuba, 8, 10, 41

Cultural pluralism, 34–35, 78–
    79
Culture, world, 77–138
Curtis, Lionel, 51

Darwin, Charles Galton, 13,
    93–94
Dehumanization, 8, 20–22
Democracy, world, 142–44
Denmark, 104
Doxiadis, Constantinos, 18

Ecocide, 8, 15–19, 25, 45,
    154–55
Ecological planning, 155–58
Ecology, 16–17, 145
Economy, world, 140–42,
    151–61
Education, 121–38, 145, 149,
    161
Egypt, 8
Elites, revolutionary, 49–50
Ellul, Jacques, 5, 19, 20–21
Enlightenment, 78
Evil, 96
Existentialism, 90–91, 96

Fabius, Quintus, 57
Falk, Richard, 74
Families, 6, 114–18, 157
Federalism, world, 32–35, 51,
    59, 143
Fellini, Federico, 87
Fellowship of Reconciliation, 31
Feminine mystique, 101–02
Fischer, John, 37
France, 44, 104, 143
Freud, Sigmund, 109
Friedan, Betty, 101
Fromm, Erich, 6
Fuller, Buckminster, 37–38,
    155
Functionalism, 35

Galbraith, John Kenneth, 158
Galtung, Johan, 15
Gandhi, Mohandas K., 31
Germany, 8, 9, 20, 104, 134
Goethe, J. W. von, 90
Government, world, 140–46,
    161
Grant, G. Gray, 59–60
Great Britain, 31, 104
Greece, 84, 90
Group marriage, 116–18

Hammarskjöld, Dag, 58
Harrington, Michael, 5
Heard, Gerald, 53, 56
Heidegger, Martin, 130
Hinduism, 56, 84
History, 137–38
Hocking, William Ernest, 51,
    52, 56
Homosexuality, 111–12
Hudson, Richard, 59

Hudson Institute, 119
Hughes, H. Stuart, 10
Hughes, Howard, 158
Hutchins, Robert M., 51, 146
Huxley, Aldous, 21
Huxley, Julian S., 34, 51

India, 8, 9, 29, 61, 63, 65, 83,
    84, 89, 154
Indochina, 8, 31
Ireland, 58
Islam, 56
Israel, 8, 118

Japan, 8, 14, 31, 61, 64, 81,
    153
Jaspers, Karl, 19
Jesus, 12, 89–90, 97
Jews, 3, 9, 82
Jonas, Gerald, 16–17
Judiciary, world, 146
Jung, Carl Gustav, 95

Kahler, Erich, 19, 51, 135
K'ang Yu-wei, 51
Kant, Immanuel, 51, 147
Kashmir, 9
King, Martin Luther, 31
Korea, 8, 9
Korzybski, Alfred, 36

Langer, William, 13
Law, world, 146–51
League of Nations, 32
Lenin, V. I., 57
Lessing, G. E., 121

Mannes, Marya, 103–04
Maoism, 24
Marcuse, Herbert, 111–12,
    119–20
Maritain, Jacques, 52
Marx, Karl, 60, 159
Marxism, 24, 78, 167
Mead, Margaret, 70
Mendlovitz, Saul, 73
Meyer, Cord, Jr., 51
Mill, John Stuart, 114, 116
Morality, world, 90–96
Morgenthau, Hans, 33
Mormonism, 56
Morris, Charles W., 56
Mumford, Lewis, 19, 51, 162
Mussolini, Benito, 106

Nationalism, 42–43, 154
Nature, 165–67
Neurath, Otto, 135
New Left, 40–45, 49, 72
New Zealand, 140
Nietzsche, Friedrich, 22, 54,
    90–91, 165–66
Nihilism, 8, 22–24
Northrop, F. S. C., 51